FORD MODEL T

The Car That Put the World on Wheels

Lindsay Brooke
in cooperation with The Henry Ford
Forewords by Bill Ford, Executive Chairman, Ford Motor Company
and Patricia Mooradian, President, The Henry Ford

MOTORBOOKS

First published in 2008 by Motorbooks, an imprint of MBI Publishing Company, 400 First Avenue North, Suite 300, Minneapolis, MN 55401 USA

Motorbooks titles are also available at discounts in bulk quantity for industrial or sales-promotional use. For details write to Special Sales Manager at MBI Publishing Company, 400 First Avenue North, Suite 300, Minneapolis, MN 55401 USA.

To find out more about our books, join us online at www.motorbooks.com.

Library of Congress Cataloging-in-Publication Data

Brooke, A. Lindsay.
  Ford model T : the car that put the world on wheels / by Lindsay Brooke.
    p. cm.
  ISBN-13: 978-0-7603-2728-9 (hardbound w/ jacket)
  1. Ford Model T automobile—History. I. Title.
  TL215.F75B76 2008
  629.222'2--dc22
                                                2007043891

Front cover: In researching the history of his '09 Touring, John Forster found that the car had fallen derelict by the early 1930s. It was fully rebuilt by a Ford dealer who wanted to keep his mechanics employed during the Depression. The car's body, featuring aluminum panels, was made by the Pontiac Body Company, one of Ford's suppliers. The step surface of the early wooden running boards was linoleum. *Jim Frenak/FPI Studios*

Frontispiece: Ford and his small team designed the T's engine to be as efficient to manufacture as it was to operate. Its removable cylinder head was an industry first. In this circa-1916 factory photo, the 2.9-liter engine's front valve-chamber cover is removed to show the valve gear. The Kingston carburetor on this engine appears to combine the body of a Model Y "four-ball" 4400, used on 1913–1914 cars, with the bowl of a Model L from 1915–1917. Other carbs came from Buffalo and Holley. *From the collections of The Henry Ford*

Title pages: From its inception in April 1908 (four months before the Model T entered production), the company-published *Ford Times* chronicled the amazing feats of the automaker's products in the hands of everyday people around the world. It also reported Ford news and service information. This whimsical illustration of a rather chaotic all-Ford world in 1917 was probably not far from Henry Ford's own mindset. Note the road signs, the wrecked motorcycle sidecar rig, and the tongue-in-cheek "Tea Gardens" on the pub's awning. *From the collections of The Henry Ford*

Editor: Dennis Pernu
Designer: Kou Lor

Printed in China

CONTENTS

FOREWORDS

On June 16, 1903, a 39-year-old Detroit businessman named Henry Ford formed a company to build and sell automobiles. His business plan was simple: he wanted to make cars affordable for the average family.

Within a few short years, his simple idea changed the world.

To fully appreciate the impact my great-grandfather had on people's lives, you have to understand what life was like when he started his company. In 1903, there were only 8,000 cars in the United States and less than 150 miles of paved road. The average wage was 22 cents an hour. Most people rarely traveled more than 25 miles from home in their entire lifetime.

To build cars for what he called "the great multitude," Henry Ford worked on a series of progressively better-designed and lower-priced cars. Finally, in 1908, he introduced his automotive masterpiece: the Model T. Within a few years he had adopted the moving assembly line and the five-dollar-day, innovations that helped create and define the industrial age. This remarkable combination of vision, process, and product put the world on wheels and began modern life as we know it.

The Model T was simple, affordable, and reliable. It changed the way we live, work, and play, providing mobility and prosperity on an undreamed-of scale. In time, it became an integral part of everyday life, popular culture, and even our language.

Whether you call it the Tin Lizzie or the Car of the Century, 100 years after its introduction, the Model T is assured of its place in history—and in the hearts of automotive enthusiasts around the world.

—Bill Ford
Executive Chairman, Ford Motor Company

In E. B. White's famous 1936 essay, "Farewell to Model T," he wrote that the Model T was "like nothing that had ever come to the world before." Henry Ford's simple idea—to make an affordable car—changed our world in ways that no one could have ever predicted.

This sturdy, useful car that farmers and working people alike could afford to buy and the modest man behind it drove the transformation of the landscape, the economy, and the social fabric of America.

At The Henry Ford, we use our sometimes rare, sometimes ordinary artifacts from America's past to tell stories of American ingenuity, innovation, and resourcefulness. And we do so to inspire current and future generations to make innovative contributions of their own, to be active change agents, and to help create a better world. We achieve this goal by telling the stories of the people behind the artifacts—the dreamers, the designers, the risk-takers, and the creators of the things that have made this country great.

People like Henry Ford and his Model T.

—Patricia Mooradian
President, The Henry Ford

INTRODUCTION

The Most Important Car in History

The impact of Henry Ford and his Model T

The first hints of spring were in the air when Henry Ford affirmed the course that set his name, and that of his latest product, on the path to immortality.

On this April morning in 1909, Ford's three-story factory on the corner of Piquette Avenue and Beaubien in Detroit was humming with energy. The state-of-the-art plant was packed with cars in various stages of assembly. From his second-floor office, Ford was in the center of the action—between the engine-machining equipment on the plant's ground floor and the final assembly shop on the third floor.

Not far beyond his office walls the car bodies were mated to their chassis amid an endless soundtrack of tools ringing against metal. From his desk, Ford caught whiffs of fresh paint, rubber tires, and tanned-leather upholstery, as well as petroleum, grease, and human sweat—an intoxicating aroma that permeated the immense brick building.

And the mood throughout the place was bright indeed. Ford had been building the new Model T for seven months, and the car was a bona fide hit in the marketplace. Indeed, the avalanche of advance orders received prior to the car's launch

The famous Greenfield Village, part of The Henry Ford historical and education complex in Dearborn, Michigan, operates the world's largest fleet of Model Ts in regular use. Comprising mostly Touring models, the cars haul visitors year-round and are maintained by a devoted group of enthusiast experts. The fleet includes restored cars as well as Centennial Ts (one of which is pictured here) built new by Ford Motor Company in 2003 to celebrate the automaker's 100th anniversary. *Ford Motor Co.*

The advertising slogan "Watch the Fords Go By" was lived daily in the United States during the 1910s and 1920s, when Ford commanded roughly half of the auto market and the streets were filled with black "flivvers." This 1924 marketing photo taken in Highland Park shows the year's model range: the two-door sedan and TT truck in the foreground, with a four-door Touring, and Roadster behind. *From the collections of The Henry Ford*

meant the first full year of Model T output was virtually spoken for already.

Customers were snapping up the two most popular variants at a faster rate than Ford's 2,000 workers could build them. The $850 Touring, its five-passenger open body painted in bright Carmine Red (soon to be joined by elegant Brewster Green), was the hottest seller. It was accompanied by the $825 two-seat Runabout, available in gray only. A town car ($1,000), coupe ($950), and landaulet ($950) were also in the works.

The T was validating Ford's growing reputation as a producer of durable, reliable automobiles that delivered good value, although $850 was the average annual salary of an American schoolteacher in 1909.

In the five years since its 1903 founding, the Ford Motor Company had produced approximately 28,000 cars. The products had evolved from the tiny twin-cylinder, chain-driven Model A through an alphabet-soup of Models B, C, F, K, N, R, and S. The most recent offerings, the N, S, R, and K, were superseded when Henry Ford placed his bet on the T.

In terms of sheer output, Ford already was the brand to beat among the 45 automobile makers operating in Michigan,

The inscription in blue ink on the back of this July 1921 print reads, "Rear view of stuck Rolls-Royce." The Model T, owned by Chester Mathias of Del Norte, Colorado, was photographed extracting the Rolls out of axle-deep mud near Holbrook, Arizona. The British luxury car was on a cross-country test but was unprepared for the rural U.S. roads of the period. The T's light weight, low gearing, and tall, skinny tires—3x30 inches in the front and 3 1/2x30 inches in the rear—allowed it to traverse rutted roads previously fit only for horses. *From the collections of The Henry Ford*

Promotional and marketing photographs of the various T models were usually static poses to accommodate the cameras and long-exposure film of the day. Jaunty new Ts, such as this brass-radiator 1915 Coupelet, looked comfortably at home in the leafy Michigan towns that often provided atmospheric backgrounds. Even with its reverse-hinged door, a Coupelet was a tight squeeze for most drivers. Note the adjustable windshield. *From the collections of The Henry Ford*

25 of them in Detroit alone. It also was top producer among the hundreds of companies in the United States then engaged (with varying degrees of success) in the high-stakes business of "automaking."

But in early 1909, the nascent T was still very much a work in progress. Nearly each of the 2,500 examples built since the documented "first" production car on September 27, 1908, differed in some way from the others. Part redesigns were incorporated on the fly. Features were added and removed as the company's founder and his small team of engineers and draftsmen amended their drawings and reconfigured the wooden molds and patterns.

At the same time, dealers were already calling for the 46-year-old "Mr. Ford" to expand his model range beyond

There was no such thing as "typical" duty for the Tin Lizzie because it did nearly everything—and did it well. For many years the T was called upon to bridge the gap between rural farm life and the town or city. The family goat and young passenger seem to be enjoying the ride, circa early 1920s. *From the collections of The Henry Ford*

the new T. They believed a broader selection of vehicles, particularly with more power and amenities, would bring greater sales and higher profit. The dealers echoed a prevailing wisdom that still predominates in today's auto industry.

Many critics and "industry experts" also believed low-priced meant cheap. There was no future in selling inexpensive cars, and Ford would go broke if he tried, they asserted. But more models and upscale intensions weren't in the cards. Henry Ford had learned a hard lesson from the problem-plagued Model K—his ill-advised foray into pricier six-cylinder cars.

His mind was made up. Ford was confident he knew exactly what the mainstream customer wanted.

"Buyers are learning how to buy," he reflected in *My Life and Work*, a semi-autobiographical book written in 1922 by journalist Samuel Crowther with Ford's input and review. "The majority will consider quality and buy the biggest dollar's worth of quality.

"If, therefore, you discover what will give this 95-percent of people the best all-round service and then arrange to manufacture the very highest quality and sell at the very lowest price, you will be meeting a demand which is so large that it may be called universal."

So, on that spring day, the self-taught practical engineer and commonsense businessman set in stone his visionary plan for the "universal car" that would soon transform personal

Averaging about two cents a mile in daily use, Ford cars are a necessity to every business man, doctor, salesman or farmer. And they serve the family just as well. Every man is his own mechanic with a Ford. No need of high-priced experts. And "Ford After-Service for Ford Owners" is a good thing to remember.

Buyers will share in profits if we sell at retail 300,000 new Ford cars between August 1914 and August 1915.

Runabout $440; Touring Car $490; Town Car $690; Coupelet $750; Sedan $975, f. o. b. Detroit with all equipment.

On display and sale at Ford Motor Co., 1550 Woodward Ave.

By the time this advertisement appeared in March 1915, the Model T was indeed on its way to becoming a necessity to many Americans. The copy emphasized that the Ford was so simple any owner could easily maintain it. Henry Ford delivered on his promise to share his 1914–1915 retail profits with Model T buyers upon reaching the 300,000-unit sales goal. The $50 rebate given to each of them cost the company $11 million in profits, but the scheme provided another boost to Ford's image and popularity. *From the collections of The Henry Ford*

The Model T's success spelled doom for the U.S. motorcycle industry, which during its peak in 1912–1913 included 60 different brands in production and under development. At one time Henry Ford stated publicly that he feared a lightweight, inexpensive motorcycle would outsell his Ford cars. But matched against even a semi-enclosed Model T, motorcycles lacked the car's stability and all-weather top. Families accustomed to relatively plush sidecar rigs like this four-cylinder Henderson with Goulding sidecar—made in Detroit and Saginaw, Michigan, respectively—found the reliable and increasingly affordable Model T irresistible. While his cars were helping to dig the bike industry's grave, Henry Ford himself bought a new 1917 Henderson Four with electric starting. The big, fast machine was purchased for company courier duties between Ford's Dearborn farm and the nearby Fordson tractor plant. Henry asked Henderson's president for a discount but ended up paying the $370 list price—$10 more expensive than a four-passenger Ford Touring! *Ron Rae*

mobility and, with it, modern society. As he later recalled, "I announced one morning, without any previous warning, that in the future we were going to build only one model, that the model was going to be the Model T, and that the chassis would be exactly the same for all cars."

Unquestionably from that point on the Model T, offered in multiple body styles, would be the company's only product. No more "monkeying" with the design "to spoil a good thing by changing it," Ford noted. However, none of the men with Ford that day at the Piquette plant could imagine that 18 years would pass until Ford introduced an all-new model!

Beginning approximately with serial number 2,500, the Model T's basic architecture was "frozen," as today's auto engineers describe the process of locking in a standardized design. Through the next two decades, however, scores of changes were made to the car. Some of them, particularly the optional electric starter and generator introduced in 1919 on closed cars only, were significantly useful upgrades.

The factory that shook the world—Ford's Highland Park plant, as seen at night, circa 1918. F-O-R-D was spelled out between the five giant smoke stacks of the on-site power plant and could be seen from many miles away. Industrialists and engineers the world over beat a path to this cutting-edge complex to witness the mass-production revolution. *From the collections of The Henry Ford*

A Touring body is dropped onto its chassis at Highland Park in May 1923. The car is fitted with the newly designed "one-man top," so named because it could be erected with relatively little fuss by one person. Also new on the '23 Touring was a slightly sloped windshield. Electric starting and lighting were still options 15 years after the T's introduction. *From the collections of The Henry Ford*

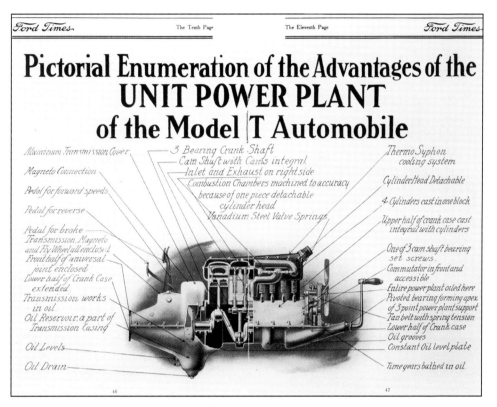

Pictorial Enumeration of the Advantages of the
UNIT POWER PLANT
of the Model T Automobile

Aluminum Transmission Cover

Magneto Connection

Pedal for forward speeds

Pedal for reverse

Pedal for brake

Transmission, Magneto and Fly Wheel all enclosed

Front half of universal joint enclosed

Lower half of Crank Case extended

Transmission works in oil

Oil Reservoir a part of Transmission Casing

Oil Levels

Oil Drain

3 Bearing Crank Shaft

Cam Shaft with Cams integral

Inlet and Exhaust on right side

Combustion Chambers machined to accuracy because of one piece detachable cylinder head

Vanadium Steel Valve Springs

Thermo Syphon cooling system

Cylinder Head Detachable

4 Cylinders cast in one block

Upper half of crank case cast integral with cylinders

One of 3 cam shaft bearing set screws

Commutator in front and accessible

Entire power plant oiled here

Pivoted bearing forming apex of 3 point power plant support

Fan belt with spring tension

Lower half of Crank Case

Oil grooves

Constant Oil level plate

Time gears bathed in oil

Nearly indestructible, easily and cheaply serviced, and full of innovation, Ford's 2.9-liter (176.7-ci) inline four-cylinder engine was rated at 22 horsepower. Bore and stroke were 3.75x4 inches. The powerplant featured a removable cylinder head and cylinders cast as part of the crankcase, both novel items in 1908. The first 2,500 engines built had water pumps, but every T made thereafter was pumpless, incorporating Ford's thermo-siphon cooling system shown in this 1909 illustration. A magneto integrated into the flywheel generated ignition and electrical power. This is one of the most important automobile powerplants of all time. *From the collections of The Henry Ford*

Other changes were made to various parts to make them more robust. Ford even eliminated the engine's troublesome gear-driven water pump, replacing it with a simple thermo-siphon system that proved extremely reliable. But the overall strategy was to optimize the basic chassis, powertrain, and underpinnings for efficient high-volume production.

By boosting his workers' productivity and driving down cost while maintaining good quality, Ford would keep his sole product imminently affordable. The T had become the franchise, and the 10,607 cars Ford sold in 1909, an industry record, were only a fraction of the tidal wave that was soon to come.

Production essentially doubled year to year, as the moving-assembly-line principles first explored at Piquette Avenue were fully deployed at Highland Park, Ford's crucible of mass production that opened in 1910. Greater output brought about by more efficient processes and automated machinery allowed Ford to steadily reduce the labor time required to build each car, thus contributing to lower retail prices.

Ford Motor Company didn't invent the moving production line; meatpackers applied it first. Ford's revolution combined a moving line and the concept of interchangeable parts in a continuous-flow system, dedicated to building one product in high volume. In doing so, he established the high-value/low-cost model that dominates the production of goods and services today.

In 1910, the basic Model T Runabout sold for $950. In 1915, the price had plummeted to $490. Five years later, it reached its best-ever price of $290. Such rock-bottom prices knocked the legs out from underneath the motorcycle-sidecar business and helped put to rest all but a few players in the once-vibrant U.S. motorcycle industry. Bikes and sidecar rigs simply could not compete with Ford's four-wheeled value.

Of the T, Henry Ford commented, "It will be so low in price that no man making a good salary will be unable to own one." Further, his company's famous "five-dollar day" living-wage profit-sharing policy, introduced at Highland Park in 1914, helped create thousands of Ford customers through a *continued on page 17*

THE FIVE-DOLLAR DAY
Ford's societal blockbuster

On January 5, 1914, Henry Ford shocked the world by announcing that his company would more than double its average worker's daily pay, which at the time was $2.34. In the same announcement, Ford added that the workday had been trimmed from nine hours to eight. Thus was born the landmark "five-dollar day"—in actuality a $10 million profit-sharing plan—that impacted society and business on an even broader scale than Ford alone.

The working man loved it, and Ford became an instant folk hero to millions, although the five-dollar day came with strings attached. Business leaders generally hated it, calling Henry Ford a socialist (and other slurs) and claiming that Ford's revolutionary move would spell doom for capitalism worldwide.

But the roots of Ford's decision were deeper than just paying his workers a wage that allowed them to afford the products they built. Ford was a founding member of the Employers' Association of Detroit (EAD), an organization formed to bargain collectively with labor unions. As it grew stronger, the EAD's mission changed to strikebreaking. (The EAD later evolved into today's much-respected American Society of Employers, which provides job training, industry research, lobbying, and consulting.)

The association served as a personnel office for many of its member companies, and one of its functions was to keep a file of "scab" (declared non-union) labor in case of a strike. It also kept dossiers on union sympathizers and others considered "troublemakers."

In June 1913, a workers' rights group called the Industrial Workers of the World (IWW), or "Wobblies," arrived in Detroit to recruit members for its cause. The organization quickly struck Studebaker's plant, calling for reforms that included an eight-hour day for factory workers. It was the first mass strike in automotive history.

Much of the work in Ford's high-volume production was tedious, monotonous, or hazardous. This is the wiring harness subassembly department, circa 1914. *From the collections of The Henry Ford*

Detroit police arrested strikers, and the EAD helped ensure no strikers were hired at other companies.

The Wobblies left Detroit but vowed to return in 1914 with Ford as their strike target. At the time, conditions were harsh on the new Highland Park assembly line, particularly in the extremely dirty jobs, such as foundry work and the paint shop. Turnover at the plant was more than 350 percent, meaning Ford had to hire more than 50,000 workers to maintain a workforce of 13,000.

The high turnover, the threat of IWW interference, and the looming strike worried Henry Ford greatly. He realized he needed a labor strategy, thus the eight-hour, five-dollar day was born. With it, Ford successfully preempted a potentially ugly and costly battle with the Wobblies.

The day after Ford announced the new wage and hours, more than 10,000 people flocked to Highland Park in search of jobs. Many of them came from lower-paying companies in Detroit. Ford couldn't handle the flood of applicants, so it closed its employment office. Finding themselves shut out in icy-cold temperatures, the job seekers responded by rioting until the Detroit Fire Department arrived and doused them with fire hoses.

Following the five-dollar day's rocky start, Ford deepened his involvement with the EAD. He encouraged its labor bureau to screen prospective Ford factory workers in an attempt to weed out union sympathizers and defectors from lower-paying companies.

To be eligible for the high pay, Ford employees first had to pass a six-month probationary period. They were expected to demonstrate that they were "sober, saving, steady, industrious, and must satisfy the superintendent and staff that his money will not be wasted in riotous living." Ford workers also were expected to meet stringent production quotas with minimal break time.

It was the responsibility of Ford's Sociological Department to prove to management that each employee either met or did not meet the prescribed requirements. The department, under the fair, level-headed John R. Lee, was established to administer the wage requirements and "promote employee welfare." To do this, an investigative arm of the department was established. At the peak of its activity, half of the department's approximately 160 men were engaged in investigating the lives of Ford employees to make sure they maintained Ford's high moral and social standards.

According to historian Ford Bryan, the Sociological Department "was given wide authority over pay increases and discharges. The rule: 'No man was to be discharged until every possible effort had been made, and every means exhausted, toward lifting him up to the requirements of the Company, and to the equal of his fellow men.'"

At the time, Highland Park was a melting pot of first-generation immigrants, many of them speaking no English. Few had the discipline or skills to properly budget their paychecks and establish savings. The Sociological Department offered English lessons, free legal services, and investment and real estate assistance.

On Henry Ford's directive, special attention was given to finding jobs for deaf, blind, and crippled applicants at all of Ford's plants. Even paroled criminals were hired when possible, as Ford believed in work as rehabilitation.

Ford was also a pioneer in hiring African Americans. During the 1920s, more than 10,000 blacks were employed at Highland Park and other U.S. Ford plants, many of whom were working in high-paid assembly jobs. Some rose to foreman and supervisory positions, with full latitude to hire and fire white workers.

Building Model Ts at Highland Park was not an easy career. But Ford employees, on average, were extremely proud of their jobs and the company. On Saturday nights in Detroit, it was common to see Ford badges pinned to the lapels of workers out on the town, as well as in churches on Sunday mornings.

The Model T's flywheel magneto and two-speed planetary transmission were a study in compactness. The entire unit was totally enclosed, unlike many period automobile power units, and thus stayed relatively clean. Planetary gearsets were fairly common on pre-1910 American cars, and Henry Ford had used them on his previous models. He believed in keeping his vehicles simple and refused to adopt the more capable sliding-gear-type transmissions until the 1928 Model A. The T's pedal-and-lever controls helped countless new drivers make the switch from the horse-drawn age to the modern automotive world. *From the collections of The Henry Ford*

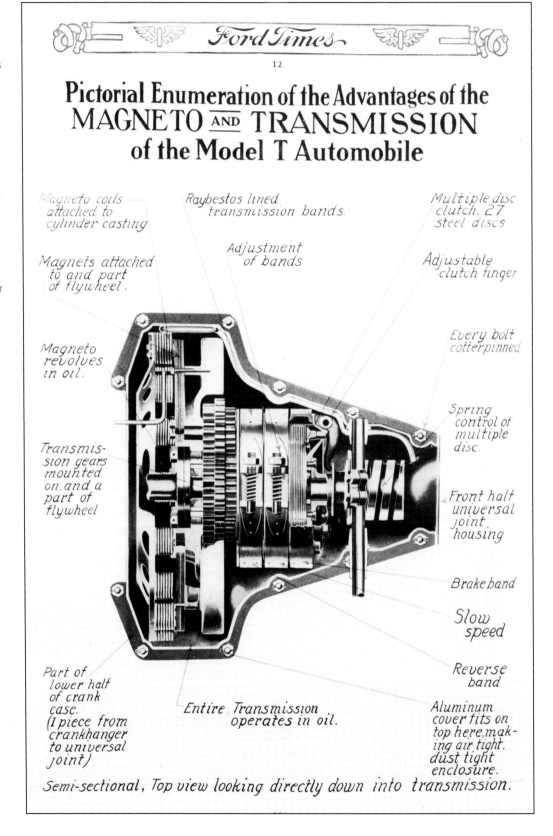

Ford Times

12

Pictorial Enumeration of the Advantages of the MAGNETO AND TRANSMISSION of the Model T Automobile

Magneto coils attached to cylinder casting

Magnets attached to and part of flywheel.

Magneto revolves in oil.

Transmission gears mounted on, and a part of flywheel

Raybestos lined transmission bands.

Adjustment of bands

Multiple disc clutch, 27 steel discs

Adjustable clutch finger

Every bolt cotterpinned

Spring control of multiple disc.

Front half universal joint housing

Brake band

Slow speed

Reverse band

Part of lower half of crank case. (1 piece from crankhanger to universal joint)

Entire Transmission operates in oil.

Aluminum cover fits on top here, making air tight, dust tight enclosure.

Semi-sectional, Top view looking directly down into transmission.

A Touring owner and his family stop to visit while out on a Sunday drive in early summer 1915. The upper half of the car's windshield is folded down, a welcome feature on a hot day. The Model T gave mobility to millions of rural folk, greatly extending their social and business worlds. *From the collections of The Henry Ford*

continued from page 13
decent base pay while raising the ire of Ford's capitalist peers (see pages 14–15).

When Henry Ford celebrated his 60th birthday in 1923, Model T output reached its zenith: 2.2 million cars built in a single fiscal year. That total equaled 57 percent of all the cars assembled in the United States.

With the internationalization of the Ford Motor Company, the Model T not only put America on wheels, but also much of the world, too. After establishing Ford of Canada in 1904, Henry Ford began building cars in Great Britain in 1911 and in Brazil in 1919. By the time production started in Australia and Germany in 1925, the humble T accounted for approximately half the world's total car production. The early advertising slogan, "Watch the Fords Go By," was manifested on streets and byways around the globe.

Seas of Model Ts were photographed streaming out of Highland Park, and Henry Ford's name became synonymous with progress. As his car struck a loud chord in the American heartland, he was widely esteemed as a populist folk hero, a social reformer (the five-dollar day is credited with helping to create the American middle class), and the most prominent industrialist in America.

Long before the era of portable generators and even rural electricity, the most readily available power source was often the drive axle of a Model T. Like the Willys Jeep many years later, the T spawned a thriving aftermarket of conversion kits. Shown in Minnesota in 1919 is a Runabout equipped with the popular Staude Mak-A-Tractor kit, complete with solid steel rear wheels and a belt-drive power takeoff. A safety guard for that fearsome circular saw was not part of the package, however. *From the collections of The Henry Ford*

The World Imitates Ford

Outside the Ford empire, the T's influence was undeniable. Automakers aspiring to volume sales created their own vehicles that mimicked the Model T's design simplicity while adopting moving-assembly-line-based production.

England's spindly Austin 7 was dubbed "the British Model T." In Italy, Fiat's 1912 Tipo Zero was company founder Giovanni Agnelli's response to the low-priced American car. His Lingotto factory, completed in 1919, was Fiat's Highland Park.

Soon after seizing power in Germany in 1933, Ford admirer Adolf Hitler enlisted Ferdinand Porsche to create a "people's car" aimed at doing for Germany's workers what the T had done for Americans. The new Volkswagen company borrowed from the Ford blueprint and even hired away 20 Ford technicians to oversee setup of the Wolfsburg factory.

Henry Ford's achievements also were studied in Japan. Kiichiro Toyoda and his brother, Eiji, whose company made automatic textile looms, dreamed of building their own car for the masses. They witnessed the Model T's rugged performance in the aftermath of the Great Kanto Earthquake that leveled most of Tokyo in September 1923.

With the majority of the city's few motor vehicles then in use destroyed in the disaster that killed more than 90,000, the Japanese government purchased 800 Model T chassis and fitted them with bus bodies for use in Tokyo's decimated transit system.

In 1925, Ford established Ford Motor Company–Japan and opened a factory there. It assembled 8,000 Model Ts per year from parts kits shipped from Detroit. General Motors arrived two years later, the American automakers bringing the first volume production to Japan's fledgling auto industry.

Kiichiro Toyoda pored over *My Life and Work* and visited America to observe operations in Detroit first-hand. What he learned helped pave the way for the creation of the Toyota Motor Company in 1936.

While Toyota erroneously often gets credit for the concept of just-in-time production, Ford pioneered the practice in 1916. Highly integrated materials ordering, parts deliveries, and assembly scheduling at the Henry Ford and Son tractor factory in Dearborn drove some of the lowest inventories and production costs in the industry.

"To some extent, every carmaker in this century has borrowed from Ford's genius," observed veteran auto industry

Ford Times often collaborated with Ford dealers to stage thrilling displays of car performance. Climbing steps was a favorite stunt in the early days and almost always drew a large crowd. This photo was taken at the YMCA in Columbus, Nebraska. *From the collections of The Henry Ford*

analyst Maryann Keller in her 1993 book, *Collision: GM, Toyota, Volkswagen and the Race to Own the 21st Century.*

Model T production finally ceased in May 1927 after more than 15 million examples had rolled out of Ford's vast assembly network. Its record as history's most prolific vehicle was unmatched for five decades, until it was broken by VW's Type 1 Beetle in 1972. Ironically, both vehicles remained in production for too long, their makers refusing to accept that time and competitors had made them obsolete.

"One sees them all about—men who do not know that yesterday is past, and who woke up this morning with their last year's ideas," asserted Ford in *My Life and Work*. "There is a subtle danger in a man thinking that he is 'fixed' for life. It indicates that the next jolt of the wheel of progress is going to fling him off."

This, of course, is exactly what happened to Henry Ford when he refused to develop a successor to the T by the mid-1920s.

Car of the Century

When it came time to choose the most significant, influential, and memorable motor vehicle of the twentieth century, a group of more than 100 automotive journalists, historians, museum curators, and other auto experts from the United States, Europe, and Asia had no trouble deciding.

In December 1999, after three years of considering hundreds of famous nameplates and narrowing the list of finalists, the experts named the Model T "Car of the Century."

Ford's Tin Lizzie was the hands-down winner. Well behind it in points were the Morris/BMC Mini and the VW Beetle—the most popular heirs to the T's inexpensive, people's-car legacy. (The Beetle remains the all-time volume king, with 21.5 million units built from 1945 to 2003, but its annual-production peak of 1.3 million cars in 1971 fell far short of the 2.2 million Ts built in 1923.)

What was so special about a spindly-looking machine that is probably best remembered as the favorite crashmobile

In Payne, Ohio, they may still be talking about the day Joe Miller paraded 49 of his closest pals through town on his Model T. The nearly 3,500-pound payload had the leaf springs compressed to the limit of their design, but by all accounts nothing was found broken when the guys disembarked. *From the collections of The Henry Ford*

Ford's advertising copywriters were thinking very progressively when they created this 1924 ad. Women in management, particularly those who owned their own businesses, were extremely rare even during the jazzy Roaring Twenties. The text's rationale for the businessperson owning an automobile remains logical today. *From the collections of The Henry Ford*

of Laurel and Hardy, the Keystone Cops, and other slapstick comedians? Why does the car that became the definitive $20 jalopy during the Great Depression and was described by novelist John Steinbeck as having a "high and snotty" appearance remain so enduring?

The answer is the T was the technologically perfect automobile for its time.

It was developed as "a motor car for the great multitude," explained Henry Ford in 1922, and as such was sized right both for individual owners and families. And its 100-inch wheelbase accommodated many different bodies, from jaunty roadsters to commercial vans.

The T's controls were configured so any person could operate it—a key consideration during an era when few people had even ridden in a motor car, let alone driven one. Its high ground clearance, light weight, and 30x3 1/2-inch tires, propelled by a willing 22-horsepower, 176.7-ci (2.9-liter) side-valve, four-cylinder engine, enabled the car to slog through rough, deeply rutted roads with relative ease.

Cruising speed on a smooth, flat road was 35 miles per hour. Flat out, with no headwind, the T could muster 45. Even at that velocity, the car was near the limit of its modest braking power.

"They accelerate slow and decelerate even slower," observed T owner David Jones in 2006. "All braking is in the transmission. Stopping a Model T must be a planned event."

And the whole vehicle was stone-simple. Anyone with a few hand tools, some baling wire, and rudimentary mechanical

Dr. William A. Smith of Glendale, South Carolina, with his 1913 Runabout, which he purchased new from the E. F. Bell Ford agency in Spartanburg, South Carolina. The Runabout was the perfect car for doctors, who usually had to drive far and wide to visit their patients at home. Dr. Smith apparently loved his Model T because he still owned it in 1922, when this photograph was taken. *From the collections of The Henry Ford*

skill could keep it running. Hand-cranking to start it took a little practice, but owners mastered the technique quickly.

No one would argue that the Model T was aesthetically beautiful. Indeed, like the Beetle and Willys Jeep many years later, it was anti-stylish, and that was just fine with the majority of customers who loved the car for what it could do.

"Uncompromisingly erect, unquestionably ugly, funereally drab, the Model T combined the webfootedness of the duck with the agility of the mountain goat. It could go anywhere—except in society," quipped *The Antique Automobile* in 1954.

The High-Tech T

While today it is only slightly more complex than your average lawn tractor, Ford's "flivver" was packed with clever engineering, much of which was quite ambitious for a low-priced vehicle. But its technologies were proven, rather than cutting-edge. This was as Henry Ford intended.

"The Model T had practically no features which were not contained in some one or other of the previous models," Ford noted in *My Life and Work*. "Every detail had been fully tested in practice. There was no guessing as to whether or not it would be a successful model. It had to be."

Vanadium steel, which was developed in Europe and used on premium-priced vehicles and racing cars, was the most important enabling technology on the Model T. It was adopted by Ford for use in various stressed parts, including the forged front axle, wheel spindles, and crankshaft. The steel alloy, which has a tensile strength nearly three times greater than the less-expensive lower-grade steels Ford had

previously used, had been thoroughly tested on the Models N and S.

"Despite its strength it could be machined more easily than plain steel," wrote Charles Sorensen, the pugnacious manufacturing chief in his book, *My Forty Years with Ford.* "Immediately Mr. Ford sensed the great possibilities of this shock-resisting steel."

The boss, along with a coterie of technical experts—primarily chief designer C. H. Wills, design and engineering wizard Joe Galamb, metallurgist John Wandersee, and toolmaker Carl Emde—found that vanadium alloys would help them achieve a stronger, lighter, and ultimately less costly car. Less mass meant lower stress on the powertrain, axles, and springs and better overall performance. The basic 1909 Runabout weighed a mere 1,200 pounds without fuel.

The Model T's engine pioneered the use of cast-in cylinders and a removable cylinder head—mainstays of modern engines. At the time, automobile engines were built up using pairs of separate cylinder castings that were mechanically fastened into the crankcase block. Their cylinder heads and blocks were a single chunk of iron.

Not only was such a clunky design expensive and time-consuming to produce, but it also was heavier, lacked durability, and was difficult to repair and service. Ford's T engine (Sorensen credited Henry with the removable-head concept) transformed the art of engine-making.

The T's two-speed (low and high ratios) planetary transmission was as brilliantly simple as its engine. Henry Ford swore by planetary-gear transmissions. He was convinced their compact design, ease of operation, and reliability were superior to the sliding-gear types coming into vogue on other brands.

"Gearshifts in those days were brutes," noted Sorensen. "An absent-minded or an overeager driver could strip gears toothless quicker than you could say, 'Excuse my dust.'" Risk of such calamity made Ford commit to a better solution.

Ford used planetary gearsets in the original Model A and all subsequent cars through the 1927 Model T, having secured a U.S. patent (No. 787,908) for the design, reported *The Automobile* on May 6, 1905.

The first batch of Ts (estimated at 800 to 1,000 cars) featured two control pedals and two floor-mounted levers.

Ford's incomparable success with the Model T during the 1910s continued after World War I. By that time, the car was already a decade old, but Henry Ford had no intention of making major changes or developing a replacement. Here, he exudes his usual confidence, posing with a new 1921 Sedan near a Ford dealership in Buffalo, New York. The T's grandest production years were still ahead. *From the collections of The Henry Ford*

The left pedal controlled low and high gears. The right pedal applied the transmission brake, which acted on the driveshaft; it served as the main retarding device in normal operation. The two levers, at the driver's left, controlled the miniscule parking brakes at the rear wheels, plus reverse gear.

Functionally, the system was simpler than it appeared (described in detail in Chapter 4), but it proved unsatisfactory

to Henry Ford. He had Galamb redesign the setup to add a third pedal (to apply reverse gear) between the first two. At the same time, the brake lever was modified; when it was pulled back slightly, it released the high-gear clutch. Pulling it back further kept the car in neutral and applied the rear brakes.

Millions of untrained drivers found Ford's two-speed planetary to be a breeze to learn and operate. It was nearly

During its 19-year production run, the Model T was the industry's undisputed volume king and the world's most popular car. Continuous improvement to the Highland Park production process enabled fantastic output in the years after World War I—one million cars produced in 1921, and twice that many in 1923. By 1924, Ford had built 10 million Ts and used that milestone to further trumpet the car and the company. The celebrated 10 millionth embarked on a cross-country tour, with film crew in tow to record the trip. Three years later, another five million Ts were on the road. *From the collections of The Henry Ford*

Ford already had distribution and sales outlets in several countries when the Model T debuted, and the new car's blockbuster success dramatically increased the company's global footprint. The Ford dealer in Cuba advertised "The Universal Car" on this alley wall in Havana. *From the collections of The Henry Ford*

It wasn't easy to wear out a Model T, but by the late 1930s their numbers on American roads began to dwindle as more comfortable, more powerful, and better-equipped used cars of various brands became widely available. The scrap drives of World War II dramatically reduced the number of Ts that were sitting in junkyards or rusting behind barns and garages. Still, thousands of Tin Lizzies remained in unconventional use, as this derelict Fordor powering a Louisiana oil derrick in 1941 proves. *From the collections of The Henry Ford*

impossible to grind the gears. And in a panic situation applying any one pedal, or a combination of them, would slow or stop the car.

"This was a remarkable transmission," reflected Sorensen. As many T owners will confess, the car can be gently rocked back and forth simply by stepping on and off the low and reverse pedals in succession. T owners used this technique in countless situations to keep the car from getting stuck.

Ford's design team aimed to keep the powertrain tidy, so they enclosed the engine, transmission, flywheel, and universal joint within a one-piece stamped steel cover. In addition, the internal parts were lubricated automatically by a splash-and-gravity oil system so the T owner didn't have to bother with messy external oil cups and hand pumps.

Today, sealed powertrains are standard fare, but on the 1909 Ford it was forward-thinking engineering that kept the car cleaner than many of its oil-spitting contemporaries. (On early production Ts, steel stampings also were used on the car's rear-axle housing; although the parts were soon changed for stronger castings, the stampings were a breakthrough in terms of their complexity.)

Having grown up on a farm, Henry Ford wanted the T to be capable of traversing furrowed fields and rutted rural roads. That requirement inspired the so-called three-point suspension system, in which the engine/transmission unit and front and rear axles were mounted in a triangular configuration, atop transverse leaf springs located fore and aft. This setup allowed the chassis to flex without twisting the engine and provided ample axle movement when the going got rough.

The T's three-point setup was influenced by Ford's bad experience with the ill-fated Model K. That big car's frame flexed so much over potholes that it often fractured or broke the mounts off the engine's aluminum crankcase. It is said that because of this fault, Henry Ford shuffled chief engineer Childe Harold Wills away from primary development work on the T, replacing him with the superbly capable Joe Galamb.

Other Model T innovations included the first use of left-hand drive in a major automobile (spearheading the move by the rest of the U.S. auto industry) and the flywheel magneto. With the car's magneto built into the flywheel, the T owner didn't have to worry about a storage battery going flat because the car didn't need one for powering the ignition. The T would start in just about any condition.

Opening up the World

Ford's Model T didn't create personal mobility; the horse accomplished that centuries earlier, the bicycle and motorcycle reprised it, and other early carmakers took numerous stabs at it. But the T offered the right combination of reliability, utility, and comfort at a price that couldn't be refused.

The T's ubiquity gave rise to a host of popular jokes and songs, many of which were affectionate jabs at the homely car's unpretentiousness:

> Q: *Why is a Model T like an affinity (a 1920s euphemism for "mistress")?*
> A: *Because you hate to be seen on the streets with one.*

But owners formed lasting bonds with their Fords, much as they'd done with horses in the previous age. They marveled at how much the little car opened up their world. The Model T was more than just a car: it became part of your life. You drove it to work and carried your family in it to church and the store. You pulled wagons and made deliveries. Or maybe you just tore down a country road for the pure joy of it.

When the horse and buggy were the prime movers in rural America, a trip to a town 20 miles away was a full day's journey. During the Model T's reign, miles traveled by car rose steadily. Today, Americans average 10,000 miles traveled by car each year.

Led by the Model T, the automobile rapidly swept nineteenth-century agrarian America away in a rising tide of high-spoked wheels, shiny black paint, and Klaxon horns, and replaced it with a vastly transformed twentieth-century industrial scene.

The impact of the automotive explosion sparked by the Model T also includes many of the societal, infrastructure, and environmental challenges facing the world today.

By 1932, nearly one out of every five Americans owned a car, and more than 22 million vehicles were on U.S. roads (with Ts still counting for a significant number of them). A U.S. government study entitled "Recent Social Trends in the United States" concluded that "Car ownership has created an 'automobile psychology'; the automobile has become a dominant influence in the life of the individual, and he in a real sense has become dependent upon it."

The Model T and other affordable cars sparked the expansion of the road system and parking spaces to cope with them, and a dramatic population shift from urban to suburban living.

Author Mary Cahill, in her book *Carpool: A Novel of Suburban Frustration* (1991), describes an affliction of automobile-dependent family life: carpool fatigue. It's the result of drivers spending their days creeping along traffic-choked roads, on and off the brakes, enduring shrill horns and rude gestures, all the while wasting precious time sitting in a vehicle and making little progress toward the destination.

As for the man most identified with putting the world on wheels, Cahill asserted, "If Henry Ford were alive today, I would strangle him."

Of course, ever since the first steam-powered carriages were spooking horses on city streets in the 1800s, the automobile has been both praised and damned everywhere it goes. Perhaps Ford's real impact was best summed up by Will Rogers, America's greatest sage in the first half of the twentieth century, who observed of the Model T's creator: "It will take a hundred years to tell whether he helped us or hurt us, but he certainly didn't leave us where he found us."

Henry Ford posed in 1910 with his first automobile, the 1896 Quadricycle. Steered by a tiller, the brakeless car was powered by a 59-ci twin-cylinder engine installed in a spindly chassis made of angle iron. Between 1896 and 1898, Ford used the Quadricycle and its few successors to attract financial backers for his fledgling auto company. *From the collections of The Henry Ford*

Chapter 1

BEFORE THE MODEL T

**Ford's early history and the "alphabet" cars—
Models A, B, C, F, K, N, R, and S**

Forty-five years before the car that put the world on wheels was born, the man who conceived it was himself born. The American Civil War was raging when Henry Ford took his first breath on July 30, 1863, in Dearborn, Michigan. Today the area is thickly settled suburban Detroit; then it was rural farmland, home to Henry's parents, William and Mary Ford, who owned a profitable farm and orchard in Springwells Township.

From childhood, Henry clearly displayed a strong interest in all things mechanical. He tolerated school, though not much more, and gained much of the practical wisdom that would serve him well in life from the popular *McGuffey's Readers* schoolbooks. Academia and the monotony of farming took a backseat to young Henry's love of handwork—he built a small water wheel and attempted a simple steam turbine, both projects ending in minor calamity.

At 16 years old, Henry left home to seek skills and employment in nearby Detroit, already a thriving industrial city full of machine shops, shipyards, foundries, carriage makers, sawmills, and steelworks. Although he quit his first job after less than a week, his next two places of employment—the Michigan Car Company, which built streetcars, and the James Flowers and Brothers machine shop—provided vital basic knowledge of mechanisms, tools, and shop skills.

Henry Ford never would have made it as an automaker, let alone achieved greatness, without the unwavering support of his wife, Clara. Shown here relaxing with her husband in 1910, Clara Ford exerted a quiet but firm influence on many of his decisions. When Ford refused to sign an agreement to accept unionized labor in his plants in 1941, Clara told him she would leave him. Henry relented. *From the collections of The Henry Ford*

At Flowers, where he apprenticed in 1880, Henry put in 60-hour weeks for the princely wage of $2.50 per week. He bolstered his salary with a night job in the Magill jewelry store, repairing watches and clocks. It was at this time that Ford first began reading about Nikolaus Otto's landmark invention of the four-stroke gasoline engine, the details and operation of which riveted him.

Moving on, Ford took a job in the Detroit Dry Dock Company's machine shop, where he worked for two years. Occasional visits to the family farm (no doubt giving his father hopes that Henry would return permanently to the agrarian life) were interspersed with employment at the Westinghouse Engine Company, where he worked on traction engines, and

brief attendance at the Goldsmith, Bryant and Stratton Business University in Detroit.

Ford had become an accomplished machinist and mechanic, able to make parts and devise solutions and always thinking of how to improve existing designs. But his father's offer of a tract of land on which Henry could build a house brought him back to Springwells—and to Clara Bryant, a local farmer's daughter, whom he married in April 1888.

With a fine new house and workshop constructed by Henry (he had set up his own sawmill to cut the lumber), the Fords appeared to be settling into a life fairly close to the one William Ford envisioned for his son.

It wasn't to be.

After a day of repairing an Otto-type stationary engine at a local plant, Henry "sat Clara down, and told her he was convinced that such a gasoline engine could be adapted to a road-going vehicle," according to auto historian Beverly Rae Kimes in her book, *The Cars that Henry Ford Built*.

The Quadricycle Lives!

Constantly supportive of Henry's dreams, Clara was on board. In September 1891 the Fords packed up and moved to 58 Bagley Street in Detroit where Henry, set on learning all he could about electricity and how it could be harnessed to provide spark, took an engineering job at the Edison Illuminating Company. Two years later in his kitchen, he tested his first homemade gasoline engine, spinning the flywheel while Clara trickled gasoline into the intake port. The noise, smoke, and commotion must have alarmed their recently born son, Edsel.

While Ford barely avoided blowing up his house with a crude single-cylinder engine made out of gas pipe and discarded lathe parts, other inventors were already creating "horseless carriages." In 1885, Karl Benz built his first petrol-burning tricycle in Germany, using an Otto-type combustion engine. A year later, Göttleib Daimler built a four-wheeled vehicle with an engine fueled by mineral spirits. Frenchmen Édouard Delamare-Deboutteville, René Panhard, Emile Levassor, and Louis Renault were also building engines and vehicles, using the skills and processes practiced in machine shops and the flourishing bicycle industry.

In the United States in the 1890s, many forward-thinkers, including Charles and Frank Duryea, Elwood Haynes, Elmer and Edgar Apperson, Alexander Winton, Ransom Eli Olds, Hiram Percy Maxim, and James Packard, were introducing their own motorized vehicles. And not all early American cars were powered by internal combustion petrol engines—the Stanley brothers were leading proponents of steam-powered automobiles, and many others believed clean, quiet, battery-powered electrics were the future.

Henry Ford's first car was already in the works that day in March 1896 when he pedaled his bicycle behind Charles King's gasoline buggy (the first car to run in Detroit) as it popped and stuttered through the city's streets. King graciously told Ford all about his car, and Henry used the knowledge, along with advice from his Edison colleagues, in the design of his Quadricycle.

The new engine occupying the workbench in Ford's tiny shed was a parallel twin-cylinder unit with its cylinders laying horizontal, similar to the iconic John Deere "Johnny Popper" tractor engines that came much later. The twin displaced 59 ci (about 990 cc) and produced an estimated 4 horsepower. Spark and fuel mixture were provided by low-tension coil and a manually operated needle valve. At first the engine was air-cooled, but when it immediately overheated, Ford added brazed water jackets.

The engine was installed in a chassis fabricated out of angle iron and mounted on tall bicycle wheels. Power was delivered to the rear axle through a final-drive chain and sprockets. The cart-like machine had no brakes, and steering was by a tiller lever. It made its maiden voyage in the morning darkness of June 4, 1896, after Ford was forced to use an axe to "widen" his work shed's door to get the completed car out!

Over the next two years, Ford's Quadricycle and its handful of successors attracted much attention, helping Ford (by this time chief engineer at Edison) attract financial backers who wanted in on the exciting and high-risk emerging automobile business. Detroit Mayor William Maybury brought a circle of well-heeled men who offered to establish a company to produce a Ford car.

The Detroit Automobile Company was formed in 1899, and Ford resigned from his job at Edison. For better or worse, he was in the auto business full-time now and, according to all accounts, Clara remained solidly behind him. A year later, having blown $86,000 of the investors' cash in producing perhaps 20 cars, the money men dissolved the company.

Ford's response was to develop a racing car that was extremely successful not only on the track, but also in attracting

One of the first Ford Motor Company advertisements, heralding the 1903 Model A. The car's twin-cylinder engine gave it a competitive advantage over the single-cylinder automobiles of the day. And who wouldn't want a car with a removable body to make servicing easier? Ford's declarations against the Selden Patent would appear in company advertising for many years. *From the collections of The Henry Ford*

C. HAROLD WILLS
The perfectionist chief engineer

"He had a passion for mechanical design, he worked incessantly, and he possessed something of Ford's quality of vision," wrote historian Allan Nevins about Childe Harold Wills. "In short, he was just the man Ford needed."

Harold Wills (he never used his first name) was not a degreed engineer, but he was professionally trained in drafting, toolmaking, and machining. He expanded his knowledge with night schooling in metallurgy, chemistry, and engineering. Wills joined Ford in 1902 before the Ford Motor Company was founded but had worked closely with Henry before then, having helped develop the *999* and *Arrow* racecars.

He and Ford immediately bonded, both men sharing a practical approach to design and engineering challenges. During development of the early cars, Wills and Henry worked in Ford's unheated shop until late at night; according to Nevins, they sometimes put on boxing gloves and sparred a few rounds to warm up their hands so they could continue to draw and handle tools.

Wills' talent in translating his boss' rough sketches into properly dimensioned technical drawings was critical toward getting Ford cars into production. He had a strong artistic sense, and Wills' everlasting contribution to the company is the iconic Ford logo script, which he penned in 1906.

His metallurgical knowledge helped speed Ford's adoption of new materials, including the breakthrough vanadium-steel alloys that played a critical role in Model T engineering. Wills also has been

Childe Harold Wills

credited with introducing molybdenum steels to the auto industry. In later years, he spent much time in a purpose-built laboratory in Dearborn, researching new material properties and applications.

Wills was respected as a capable design engineer by all who knew him. His attention to detail made him somewhat of a perfectionist. Sorensen claimed he was high-strung and impatient, and he took credit for ideas that were not his own.

Judged with the advantage of hindsight, Wills' most controversial period appears to be during development of the Model T. Henry Ford assigned Wills' chief draftsman, Joe Galamb, to lead design engineering on the T project, while Wills handled the car's metallurgical development. Some historians believe the move indicated a downturn in Ford's confidence in his veteran chief engineer. This may have arisen from the problematic six-cylinder Model K, which was underdeveloped when it was launched.

Wills left Ford in 1919 and, together with former colleague John R. Lee, founded the town of Marysville, Michigan, named after Wills' wife Mary. His driving ambition was to start his own automobile company, and in 1921 he introduced the Wills Sainte Clair, a beautifully engineered, high-quality car that today would be considered a premium luxury vehicle. The company only survived for seven years, succumbing to the same cost, volume, and market issues that killed scores of early automakers.

The Henry Ford's Greenfield Village in Dearborn, Michigan, provides ideal photographic backdrops for special events, such as the June 1933 celebration of Ford Motor Company's thirtieth anniversary. Here, the company's founder reflects on the simplicity of a restored Model A in front of the Village's popular Eagle Tavern. Note the car's large front-mounted cooling radiator. A Model F is visible at right. *From the collections of The Henry Ford*

talented people. This included ace mechanic Ed "Spider" Huff and design engineer C. Harold Wills, both of whom would play key roles in the development of early Ford production cars and the Model T.

The racing interlude again buoyed investor confidence, and in late 1901 another group of backers created The Henry Ford Company to capitalize on his talent. Unfortunately Ford quit soon after the investors, tired of Henry's apparent inability to actually produce a car, brought in consulting engineer Henry Leland (later the founder of Cadillac and Lincoln).

It looked like Henry Ford's fledgling career as an automaker was doomed. His solution was to build another

Henry Ford saw racing as a quick way to prove the superiority of his early vehicles and attract investors. With the help of engineer Oliver Barthel and trusted mechanic Ed "Spider" Huff, he built his first racecar using a 540-ci twin-cylinder engine. In October 1901, with Huff literally hanging onto the car's running boards, Ford won a well-publicized 10-mile dirt-track race in Grosse Pointe, Michigan, against a much-favored Winton. The 26-horsepower Ford averaged 44.8 miles per hour; the victory netted Ford a $1,000 prize and boosted his reputation as a carmaker. Ford and Huff reenacted their winning form for this photo. *From the collections of The Henry Ford*

new racecar—the famous *999*. But even after it proved victorious in the hands of up-and-coming race driver Barney Oldfield, Ford put his speed enthusiasm on the back burner. It was time to get back to production-car development, and he had a design well in the works.

In August 1902 he joined with Alexander Malcomson, a very successful Detroit coal dealer who, along with his business partner James Couzens, helped organize and bankroll the Ford and Malcomson Company, Ltd. In December that year, Malcomson had a wagon shop near the railroad on Detroit's Mack Avenue rebuilt for the purpose of assembling motor cars. Finding reliable suppliers was difficult, but Ford was respected by John and Horace Dodge, who ran one of the biggest machine shops in Michigan.

The Dodge brothers agreed to supply Ford and Malcomson with enough engines, transmissions, axles, and chassis (each set worth $250) to equip 650 cars. John S. Gray, a Detroit candy maker and banker (and Malcomson's uncle), swapped the $10,000 needed to pay the Dodge brothers for 105 shares of stock and the company presidency. Other contracts went to the C. R. Wilson Carriage Company for wooden bodies and seat cushions ($68 each), the Hartford

Rubber Company for tires ($40 per set), and the Prudden Company for wheels ($26 per set).

Though Ford priced his car at $750 for the basic Run-about and $850 for the Tonneau model (with rear seat)—setting profit margins at $150 and $200, respectively—the company could not pay its bills.

Gray's confidence in the enterprise was always shaky. Until his death in 1906 he asserted that Ford's business would not last. But by 1915, when the Model T was on its ascendancy to unimagined greatness, his estate had received $10 million in dividends!

Ford's First Production Cars

On June 16, 1903, the Ford Motor Company was organized, absorbing the Ford and Malcomson Company. Ford and Malcomson shared 510 of the 1,000 shares of stock, with the remainder split among investors Gray, the Dodges, Couzens, Charles Bennett (president of the Plymouth Iron Windmill Company, maker of the Daisy air rifle), Albert Strelow, Horace Rackham, John Anderson, Vernon Fry, and Charles Woodall. All were either friends or business acquaintances of Malcomson.

The great Barney Oldfield was Henry Ford's first hired-gun race driver. He helped create Ford's fame at the wheel of two racecars built in 1902: the *999* shown here and the nearly identical *Arrow*. Both were powered by enormous 1,155-ci four-cylinder engines, one of them featuring a single overhead camshaft. In January 1903 on frozen Lake St. Clair, Ford and "Spider" Huff, in the *Arrow*, set the world's speed record of 91.3 miles per hour. *From the collections of The Henry Ford*

Of the $100,000 in stock issued, just $28,000 was paid in cash—and not in a single lump. The Ford bank balance in mid-June hovered around $14,000, but by early July it had plummeted to $223. Not a single car had been sold, and the creditors were getting very anxious. It was looking like Henry Ford was about to strike out again, maybe for the last time.

But on July 15, a Chicago dentist named Edward Pfennig became the first-ever Ford retail customer. When deposited, his check for $850 practically echoed in the nearly empty Ford company bank account. The company had its collective fingers crossed that more sales would come soon.

The situation intensified later in the month when Henry Ford was faced with the Selden Patent (see following pages), a matter that he battled throughout the next decade. That Ford refused to let the fight with Selden distract him from the business of building and selling Ford cars proved how doggedly focused he was.

continued on page 38

BATTLING THE SELDEN PATENT, 1903–1911

The Selden Patent was the most controversial issue confronting the fledgling American auto industry. In May 1879, patent attorney Henry R. Selden filed a patent for "a road-locomotive featuring a liquid hydro-carbon engine of the compression type." In effect, this was eventually interpreted as the automobile, and Selden was granted a patent in November 1895. The patent extended backward to all vehicles designed since 1879 and forward to cover those built or sold until 1912.

In late 1899, Selden sold exclusive rights to the Columbia and Electric Vehicle Company of New Jersey. Subsequently, these rights were assigned to the Electric Vehicle Company of Hartford, Connecticut, which eventually granted sublicenses to 26 manufacturers that had caved in to Selden's threats and decided it would be cheaper to join him than fight him in court. These manufacturers formed the Association of Licensed Automobile Manufacturers (ALAM), which set royalties at 1.25 percent per vehicle sold for American automakers and 1.5 percent for importers.

The royalties were paid to the Electric Vehicle Company, which then sent a cut of the proceeds to George Selden, who in turn gave the remainder to ALAM. The association made it clear, using ads in trade publications and newspapers, that anyone contemplating the production or sale of a gasoline-engined vehicle without an ALAM license had better think otherwise or else face legal action for patent infringement.

Within four years, the patent generated $1.5 million for ALAM, paid mainly by the most successful marques of the time: Cadillac, Franklin, Oldsmobile, Packard, Pope, Thomas, and Winton.

Ford initially investigated taking a license, but he was put off by the derogatory demeanor of ALAM president Frederick Smith, who labeled Ford a mere "assembler" rather than a "manufacturer." So Henry dug in his heels and, along with Panhard and Renault, refused to join the ALAM or pay it royalties. Their take-off-the-gloves intransigence triggered a lawsuit that lasted 10 years.

During the litigation, Ford forced Selden to build a replica of his car to prove it would run. This became the famous "Exhibit 89" which, *Horseless Age* reported, was barely functional. It took up to 12 minutes of continuous cranking to start, never ran more than 7 minutes at a stretch, and overheated so severely that it shot a geyser of steam out of the crankcase "at least 12 feet above the machine." The magazine was so critical of "Exhibit 89" that ALAM slammed the publication in an angry letter to the publisher.

Henry Ford and James Couzens stood up to Selden's threats in public, through a barrage of large display advertisements in many publications. One of the boldest ads carried the headline, "We are the pioneers of the GASOLINE AUTOMOBILE. Our Mr. Ford made the first gasoline automobile in Detroit and the third in the United States. His machine made in 1893 is still in use."

Of course Henry was stretching the truth, but his ad promised to protect "dealers, importers, agents, and users of gasoline automobiles" against prosecution for "alleged infringement of patents." The Ford ad also quoted two attorneys who stated that the Selden patent was virtually worthless.

Ford was so compelled to fight back against Selden and ALAM that he built a replica of the 1861 Lenoir engine and car, as an exhibit in the lawsuit. His aim was to disprove statements from a Selden witness that a non-compression (i.e., Otto cycle) engine could not be practical due to its low compression and great size. The Lenoir replica engine developed 3 horsepower at 200 rpm and was able to run 8 miles in 59 minutes through heavy New York City traffic.

Charles Duryea, the well-known automotive inventor, wrote to *Horseless Age* saying, "It is quite possible that Mr. Selden is entitled to a patent on the thing he shows and claims; but, that he is entitled to interpret his patent to cover entirely different structures that contain nothing invented by him, is not believed by those who know the facts."

In September 1909, Judge Charles Hough of the U.S. Circuit Court of New York held that the Selden Patent covered the modern automobile, though no decree was ever entered. This started an advertising war between the ALAM and Ford Motor Company. ALAM claimed it would consider action against unlicensed users, an obvious attempt to scare car buyers.

Henry Ford, on his way to selling more than 10,000 of his new Model Ts in the first year's production and with orders flooding in, responded with full-page ads announcing the issuance of a $12 million bond protecting Ford buyers. He also appealed Judge Hough's decision.

In 1911, the U.S. Circuit Court of Appeals issued a 45-page opinion that sustained the validity of the Selden Patent, but it also declared that the defendants' automobiles did not infringe upon it. *Horseless Age* printed the court's findings in a seven-page article, concluding that Selden's patent would have applied to modern automobiles had it been based on an Otto-cycle engine, which it was not.

In the end, the overall effect of Henry Ford's vigilant fight against what many Americans saw as a monopolistic conspiracy caused his public image to skyrocket, particularly among the Model T's customer base. As author Steven Watts commented in his 2005 book, *The People's Tycoon*, in the wake of the victory over Selden, Ford "began to appear as a homegrown folk hero."

George Selden's self-serving, protracted attempt to "patent" the automobile was based on his claimed intellectual property in this vehicle, which became known as the "Selden Patentwagon." *From the collections of The Henry Ford*

After the Model A, Ford introduced two new models in 1904: the twin-cylinder Model C and the company's first four-cylinder production car, the Model B. Shown here with Henry Ford in the front passenger seat (ahead of his secretary, Myrtle Clarkson), the Model B was the first Ford car to use a driveshaft. The B's large size and $2,000 price tag ran contrary to Ford's vision for his company's products. *From the collections of The Henry Ford*

continued from page 35

The car Dr. Pfennig purchased was Ford's Model A, which was the first example of Ford's "keep it simple and light" design philosophy. The car was available as a single-seat (two occupants) Runabout, and later as a Tonneau (making the car a four-seater), priced at $900.

With a 72-inch wheelbase, the Model A chassis weighed 1,250 pounds. It was powered by a 100.5-ci (1,750-cc), horizontally opposed, twin-cylinder gasoline engine of Ford's own design, mounted amidships under the seat with its crankshaft oriented transversely in the car's frame. Made entirely of iron, the engine was water-jacketed around the combustion chambers, its heads cast integrally with the cylinders. Cooling was provided by a centrifugal water pump and a large front-mounted bronze-and-copper radiator.

With 4-inch bore and stroke, the huge L-head (side valve) twin produced all of 8 horsepower at 1,000 rpm. Relative to its era, it was inherently smooth, a trademark of all horizontally opposed twins but reinforced in the Model A by an immense outside flywheel that further damped the power pulses.

Power was transferred via a cone-type clutch and two-speed planetary transmission. This type of gearbox transfers engine torque via rotating sets of small pinion gears that revolve around large central gears. The pinion gears resemble planets orbiting around the central sun, hence the transmission's name.

Planetary gearsets are extremely simple, compact, and reliable, which is why they are used in many automotive, aircraft, marine, and industrial applications. It's also why Henry Ford swore by them, using two-speed planetary gearboxes in all of his cars until he had to give way to conventional transmissions—but not until 1928.

Final drive to the 28-inch drive wheels was by roller chain and sprockets. The car was fully suspended on full-elliptic leaf springs, mounted longitudinally at each corner, and it rode as one would expect a small, short-wheelbase, leaf-sprung buggy with high-pressure pneumatic tires would ride.

The Model A could be coaxed to a spirited top speed of 25 miles per hour by those owners bold enough to try; the only semblance of a brake was a rudimentary band in the transmission.

Ford's original goal was to sell the Model A for $500, a target that the inexperienced automaker missed by a considerable mark. It cost $30,000 to develop and was a success

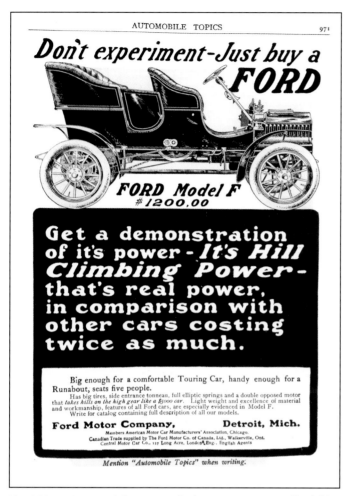

The 1905–1906 Model F was Ford's first attempt at an "affordable luxury" car. Designed to look like an expensive tourer, the $1,200 Model F actually was powered by a twin-cylinder engine and chain drive. Its "engine compartment" housed the fuel and water tanks. *From the collections of The Henry Ford*

because it did what its maker intended. In *My Life and Work* (1922), Henry Ford traced the history of the 420th Model A produced:

> *Colonel D. C. Collier of California bought it in 1904. He used it for a couple of years, sold it, and bought a new Ford. No. 420 changed hands frequently until 1907 when it was bought by one Edmund Jacobs living near Ramona in the heart of the mountains. He drove it for several years in the roughest kind of work. Then he bought a new Ford and sold his old one.*

> *By 1915, No. 420 had passed into the hands of a man named Cantello who took out the motor, hitched it to a water pump, rigged up shafts on the chassis and now, while the motor chugs away at the pumping of water, the chassis drawn by a burro acts as a buggy. The moral, of course, is that you can dissect a Ford but you cannot kill it.*

While the modest Mack Avenue plant built 1,708 Model A cars during Ford's first fiscal year (grossing $1.16 million), Henry's mind was set on far greater ambitions.

The next small step was the 1904 Model C. This was essentially a modified Model A created by adding a short section of angle iron to the front of the Model A frame and mounting the car's 9-gallon gasoline tank under a boxy hood, a major visual departure from the Model A's "curved dash" look. (The A's gas tank was under the seat adjacent to the engine and oil tank.)

Giving the Model C an actual nose stretched the car's wheelbase to 78 inches, while the advertised curb weight remained at 1,250 pounds. Engine output was boosted to 10 horsepower; final drive was still by chain. Like its earlier cousin, the Model C was built in Runabout and Tonneau versions. The advertised operating range on a tank of fuel was 180 miles.

While the first two Fords were establishing the company's product line, Henry Ford, C. H. Wills, and their small team of engineers and mechanics were considering a very different technical path. At the Detroit Automobile Show in early 1904, Ford displayed what appeared to be a new model with an air-cooled four-cylinder engine.

The inline powerplant was a major departure for Ford, with pushrod-actuated overhead valves and an aluminum crankcase. The forged-steel crankshaft ran in five main bearings, and its flywheel was mounted on the front end. Blades incorporated within the flywheel served as a cooling fan, forcing air back through and around the heavily finned iron cylinders.

The air-cooled four featured Ford's first use of a 3 3/4-inch cylinder bore, which would become the standard bore size on the Models N and T. But the car was never produced; it was just a prototype, built to test the validity of air cooling (but confirming Ford's belief that it wasn't as appropriate as liquid cooling for a car) and to establish the

The expensive ($2,500) heavyweight, six-cylinder Model K, shown here with Henry Ford and a farmhand on his Dearborn property, was everything Ford's financial backers wanted in a car, but it wasn't what Henry wanted. Built from 1906–1908, the big tourer could reach 60 miles per hour, but it quickly gained a "problem car" reputation. Today, 25 Model Ks are known to exist. *From the collections of The Henry Ford*

general dimensions and layout for the production Model B, also introduced in 1904.

The Model B, which featured a water-cooled L-head inline four, marked Ford's first use of final drive by driveshaft and bevel gears as presaged by the air-cooled show car. It was also the first to use storage batteries rather than dry-cell batteries.

The $2,000 Model B's debut marked a significant move up in overall vehicle size—and price—for Ford. A large touring car with a 92-inch wheelbase, ample 15-gallon fuel tank, and 40-mile-per-hour top-speed rating, its development was dictated by the company's directors, who believed that the route to profits was in heavier, more powerful, higher-priced cars with greater feature content. Their target customer was wealthy, no doubt about it.

That strategy was diametrically opposite of Henry Ford's vision, but what he really thought of the Model B is historically unclear. In *My Life and Work* he calls it "an extremely good car." Allan Nevins, in his essential 1954 book, *Ford: The Times, the Man, the Company*, stated that Ford "particularly disliked the Model B, upon which Malcomson had insisted."

Young Edsel Ford gets ready to take a spin with his father outside their Hendrie Avenue home in Detroit in 1905. Their ride is a new Model F, a twin-cylinder, chain-drive model with fuel and water tanks beneath its front cowling. The F was priced at $1,200, between the Models C and B. *From the collections of The Henry Ford*

According to Nevins, the move away from the $500 car, as indicated by the Model B, disturbed Henry Ford. "In 1904 the Pope-Hartford was selling for $3,200, and the five-passenger Packard, with a four-cylinder 24-hp engine was bringing $7,000," he wrote, "but Ford distrusted even a $2,000 car."

To make it a success would require some promotion on Ford's part. So on a bitterly cold winter morning, Ford, Wills, "Spider" Huff, and company metallurgist John Wandersee dusted off the old *Arrow* racecar and headed for frozen Anchor Bay on Lake St. Clair northeast of Detroit. The car's purpose here for three days was to set a new speed record that would prove a four-cylinder car's durability and power. What he didn't emphasize was the fact that the *Arrow* and the Model B engines were very different.

Ford had the snow shoveled from the glassy ice surface and set up a 4-mile course. American Automobile Association (AAA) officials were invited to time the event (they didn't arrive until the second day), and Clara and 10-year-old Edsel were present to watch. With Henry driving and Huff riding alongside as mechanic, the re-powered *Arrow* crossed the measured mile in front of the AAA men in 39.25 seconds—91.3 miles per hour.

Two ladies in a Model N motor past Ford's Piquette Avenue factory in Detroit in 1905. The spunky, robust little car accounted for most of the 8,828 units produced by the plant in 1906. The man looking out the second-story corner window is believed to be the company founder. Today, this facility is a National Historic Landmark. *From the collections of The Henry Ford*

This run stomped the previous mile record by more than 6 seconds, and Ford used the achievement in various advertising and public promotions.

"That put Model B on the map—but not enough to overcome the price advances," Ford later admitted. "No stunt and no advertising will sell an article for any length of time."

F Is for Funky

"The Model F has behind it the prestige of 'Ford Success,'" bragged the company's official sales brochure for 1905. "It is designed for Automobile users who want a practical and useful Touring car at a price which makes such as vehicle a profitable investment rather than an expensive luxury."

So this was the new F's niche: "affordable luxury," a sales hook that continues to attract car buyers more than a century later. One glance at the $1,200 Model F and it appears that Ford's company directors were twisting Henry's design arm once again. The F's looks truly were deceiving. It appeared to be front-engined, with an inline four under its sheet-metal doghouse ahead of the cowl. But on closer inspection, the louvered hood concealed not an engine but the 9-gallon gas and 4-gallon water tanks.

The car's engine was actually under the driver's seat amidships, as in the Models A and C, and it was a slightly upgraded version of those cars' opposed twin-cylinder unit, with a 1/4-inch larger bore (to give 127.2 ci, versus 113.4 in

JAMES COUZENS
Hard-nosed financial wizard

James Couzens was the business brain behind Ford's early success. He was Alexander Malcomson's bookkeeper when the Detroit coal dealer joined with Henry Ford to establish the Ford Motor Company in 1903. Couzens put up $2,500 of his own money in the venture—an investment that made him a multimillionaire when the Model T hit its stride—and was appointed the company's first secretary, responsible for all of Ford's business affairs.

"It can be presumed that Ford, by himself, could not have managed a small grocery store, and Couzens could not have assembled a child's kiddie car," observed historian Ford Bryan in his superb book, *Henry's Lieutenants*. "Yet together they built an organization that astounded the world."

Described as "one of the keenest, most experienced and most ambitious businessmen in Detroit" by Ford historian Allan Nevins, and "smart, tough, blunt, willful, and self-confident" by author Steven Watts in *The People's Tycoon*, Couzens was in charge of all of Ford's capital spending, wage decisions, dealership

James Couzens

financing, logistic strategy, and advertising from 1906 until his resignation from operations in 1915 (he remained on the company board).

He was a "dragon at the cashbox," recalled Charles Sorensen, noting that managers who went to the shrewd Couzens for spending authorization had to have their facts and data in order.

"I don't mind spending money," Couzens once replied to Sorensen's proposal for new cylinder-block casting patterns, "so long as I get something back. That's what's going to make us successful in our line."

Couzens had an explosive personality. Given to bursts of anger, he was feared by all but Henry Ford, wrote Nevins, and was known for his strict obedience to rules. After resigning from Ford in 1915 (due, to some extent, to Ford's World War I pacifist activities), Couzens launched a successful political career. He was elected mayor of Detroit in 1918. Four years later, he became Michigan's U.S. senator, an office he held for 14 years.

---

the older cars). Power was up slightly, to 12 horsepower, giving honest 35-mile-per-hour capability. Indeed, the 1905–1906 Model F resembled in many ways a pumped-up Model C. It even shared the A and C's chain final drive— likely a cost-cutting design measure compared with the Model B's more expensive-to-produce shaft drive. (Chain adjustment was made in bicycle-like manner, by loosening the rear axle and sliding it backward, tightening the chain slack in the process.)

Today's marketers might describe the Model F as a "tweener" because it slotted in Ford's three-car lineup between the twin-cylinder Model C and the four-banger Model B in weight (1,400 pounds), wheelbase (84 inches), price, and power. Even its 30-inch-diameter wheels were 2 inches larger and smaller, respectively, than those of its stable mates.

The F was available in a choice of two body styles: a two-passenger Runabout and a two-seat open Tourer. The latter body featured a roomy tonneau (backseat) that could accommodate three people on the deep black leather upholstery if necessary. Its occupants entered from the side, rather than the rear as on the Model C Tonneau, stepping up onto Ford's first running boards. The F also shared the Model B's classy forest-green and yellow-trim livery, said to have been John Dodge's idea.

As the company continued developing new models—and the next one was certainly a surprise—it should be noted that Ford Motor Company was an extremely well-run enterprise, thanks to Couzens' keen business acumen and Ford's staunch determination to avoid loans. Capital to develop new vehicles and improve the tools and plant came directly from the steadily growing sales revenue, rather than bank financing. The company was also paying its directors a healthy dividend.

Ford produced approximately 1,700 cars per year in 1903 and 1904, still far below industry leader Oldsmobile's 5,000 to 6,000 cars during the same period. But Ford's average daily output had risen to 25 cars in mid-1905, and gross sales for the fiscal year jumped to $1.91 million. Ford employed 300 people—mostly men—double the staff of the previous year. Unskilled workers earned 28 cents per hour, while machinists earned 42 cents per hour.

"So extraordinary had been the business record of the company that additional profits were available to plow back into growth," observed author Nevins of the 1903–1906 period. "The vision of a massive corporation that not only would compete with Olds, Cadillac, Buick, and others, but tower above them, had already beckoned to Ford and his associates. To fulfill his dream, a swift expansion was required and they prepared for it."

This expansion was the move into larger manufacturing quarters: the new three-story plant at Piquette Avenue and Beaubien (described in the Introduction), which opened in 1905. Ten times as large as the Mack Avenue facility, the Piquette factory was designed to be primarily an assembly plant, as most of Ford's component content was still brought in from suppliers rather than produced in-house (drivetrains and running gear still came from the Dodge brothers). The

location, in a railway nexus, was perfect for receiving freight and shipping finished cars.

Ford Springs a Six

On May 9, 1905, Detroit's evening newspapers trumpeted "Plan Ten-Thousand Autos at $400 Apiece," a headline based on Henry Ford's meeting with reporters earlier in the day. This was Ford's first public pronouncement that he intended to build a car for the masses, although he admitted, "it will take some time to figure out what we can do." A set of tires, Ford noted, cost him $60 to $70 at the time.

Unfortunately, the car being prepared for 1906 launch veered even further off into high-price, heavyweight territory. The Model K, available in Touring car or a Super-Runabout called the 640, was everything Alexander Malcomson and Charles Bennett wanted, and virtually nothing that Henry Ford desired in his motor cars.

It was the biggest Ford yet: 2,500-pound curb weight with a 114-inch wheelbase at its introduction and an added 6 inches for 1907–1908. It was the first Ford production car powered by an inline six-cylinder engine, a layout embraced by Stevens-Duryea and the air-cooled Franklin.

Ford's mighty six was a liquid-cooled L-head design featuring 4 1/2x4 1/4-inch bore and stroke. Packing an advertised 40 horsepower at 1,600 rpm and putting its power to the ground via shaft drive, the brawny K was good for 60 miles per hour.

Ford advertising trumpeted, "The whole six cylinders inspire the driver with the confidence that there is an enormous latent energy in his motor, ready for any new demand without overloading the motor, making it the easiest controlled and most flexible automobile ever built."

Such puffery probably disgusted the straight-shooting Henry Ford, but it is easy to imagine an inline six's inherent balance and smooth running appealing to Ford's innate mechanical sensibilities. It is also easy to understand the Ford directors' enthusiasm to move the model range up-market, given that approximately half of U.S. auto sales were priced at the K's level or higher. The company's 1907 catalog claimed the Model K offered "the silence of an electric with the simplicity and economy of a gasoline motor," which probably wasn't far from the truth.

Much of the K's weight came from the 405-ci engine, a massive lump with individually cast iron cylinders. In an attempt to save weight, Ford and Wills specified an enormous cast-aluminum crankcase, measuring some 50 inches long. The two-speed open planetary transmission bolted up rigidly to the flywheel, creating a long, heavy powertrain.

Henry Ford, though philosophically against the big machine, naturally had to support it in the media. Having built his reputation as a twin- and four-cylinder man, he went out of his way to argue the case for six cylinders versus four in a technical article titled "Henry Ford and the Six Cylinder" in the June 7, 1906, issue of *The Automobile*:

The two extra cylinders in the Ford K weigh, with valves and all attachments, exactly 56 pounds. The two extra pistons and rods, complete, weigh 17 pounds. The additional length of the crankshaft and aluminum base of the Six are exactly compensated for by the necessarily large diameter of those in the Four with its large bore and stroke.

We then have 73 pounds of extra weight due to the addition of the two cylinders which is however offset by 75 pounds reduction in the flywheel weight necessary for this type of motor. Credit the six with two pounds. The six cylinder motor of equal power is then 25–30 pounds lighter than the four of the same power.

While *The Automobile* called the Model K "sensational," it quickly gained a reputation as a problem car. "The frame design was too light for its running gear and engine," notes Chicago-area Ford enthusiast Don Mates, who has owned his 1908 long-wheelbase K for 40 years.

Known to many vintage Ford owners as "Dr. Flywheel," Mates explains that because of the heavy powertrain, Ford added bracing rods to reinforce the lightweight chassis. Still, the frame would flex excessively when the car was driven on potholed roads or uneven surfaces, even with its four-point engine mounting. The flexing often caused catastrophic failure of the engine-support lugs that were an integral part of the aluminum crankcases.

"The support mounts broke regularly," says Mates. "Of the 25 Model Ks that exist today, most have had their crankcases repaired at some point, or had to purchase replacement cases."

Crankshafts were also prone to breakage due to harmonic vibrations occurring at higher road speeds. These and other

HENRY FORD ON VEHICLE WEIGHT

"I had been experimenting principally upon the cutting down of weight. Excess weight kills any self-propelled vehicle. There are a lot of fool ideas about weight. It is queer, when you come to think of it, how some fool terms get into current use. There is the phrase, 'heavyweight' as applied to a man's mental apparatus! What does it mean? No one wants to be fat and heavy of body—then why of head?

"For some clumsy reason we have come to confuse strength and weight. The crude methods of early building undoubtedly had much to do with this. The old ox-cart weighed a ton—and it had so much weight that it was weak! . . .

"The most beautiful things in the world are those from which all excess weight has been eliminated. Strength is never just weight—either in men or things. Whenever any one suggests to me that I might increase weight or add a part, I look into decreasing weight and eliminating a part!

"The car that I designed [the 1903 Model A] was lighter than any car that had yet been made. It would have been lighter had I known how to make it so—later I got the materials to make the lighter car."

—Henry Ford in "Starting the Real Business," *My Life and Work* (1922)

failures caused by insufficient engineering began to harm Henry Ford's reputation and validate his belief that lightweight cars were the answer.

It quickly became apparent that Ford's Model K, although a handsome car, was a flop at $2,500 and equally so when the price was raised to $2,800. However, it was pleasant to drive: "quite nice and smooth on a smooth road, but keep it out of the rough and don't exceed 50 miles per hour," reports Mates.

Partially completed Model N chassis at the Piquette Avenue plant illustrate Ford's production capacity. The interior of the plant today is remarkably unchanged from this November 1906 photograph. The N and its close cousins, the Models R and S, flew out of Ford showrooms as fast as Piquette could assemble them. *From the collections of The Henry Ford*

One positive that did come out of the ill-fated Model K was the six-cylinder engine's use in proving alcohol as a motor fuel. In 1906, there was a movement underway to push Congress to remove the revenue duty on denatured alcohol because the price of gasoline had shot up to around 25 cents per gallon from 20 cents a few months earlier.

Most gasoline pumps were located at service garages, and garage owners (along with the Standard Oil Company) were being labeled as greedy, price-controlling monopolists, hence the early move toward alcohol as a gasoline alternative.

(In contrast to today, at that time virtually 100 percent of petroleum used in America came from oil wells in Texas, Pennsylvania, and other U.S. states.)

Anticipating the availability of alcohol to power cars, the Ford Motor Company embarked on sophisticated tests aimed at determining the best type of carburetor for vaporizing alcohol for internal-combustion engines.

"Mr. Ford states that the results have been very gratifying," reported *The Automobile*, "and that in the case of the six-cylinder type of motor, the average gasoline test of which is

52 horsepower, as high as 60 hp was obtained in several tests with alcohol as fuel."

With the Model K proving a major setback overall, Ford and Couzens were perhaps more convinced than ever that their company could profitably build inexpensive and lightweight cars. But two things had to happen to achieve that goal. First, they had to extricate themselves from the relationship with Alexander Malcomson, who had equal interest in the enterprise with Henry Ford and remained a chief proponent of large, expensive automobiles. Second, Ford Motor Company would have to manufacture its own engines, drivetrains, and—eventually—bodies.

To attend to both matters, Ford and Couzens set up a new venture, the Ford Manufacturing Company, issuing no shares to Malcomson. Although it was intended to be a manufacturing arm of the Ford Motor Company, its eventual effect was to deflate Malcomson's interest in the automobile company. In July 1906, Detroit's coal king sold his shares in the Ford Motor Company to its namesake for $175,000.

Within six months, Ford merged his two companies, and John Gray's death opened up the Ford Motor presidency. The door was open for Henry Ford to finally assume uncontested leadership of his enterprise, and he zestfully charged right through it.

Model N Takes Off

The best thing about the big, expensive Model K was the car introduced alongside it: Ford's high-value Model N. This was the car that truly set Ford on his path to the Model T.

Perfectly priced at $500, the rugged little N was packed with features. Its 149-ci, liquid-cooled, inline four-cylinder engine was mounted under the square-shaped hood in front of the driver. Like the air-cooled Model B prototype, the N's cast-iron flywheel (with fan-like spokes) was fitted on the front end of the crankshaft. Developing a claimed 15 horsepower, the engine could push the 1,000-pound car to a giddy 40 miles per hour.

The N shared its 84-inch wheelbase with the funky Model F, but it was Ford's first car to feature a transversely mounted, semi-elliptic leaf spring above the front axle—a suspension cue that would soon be a Ford trademark on the Model T.

The Model N sold like hotcakes as soon as it was announced. Demand exceeded supply, even as the price climbed to $600 in 1907, and Ford dealers were forced to take a Model K (the proverbial sack of potatoes) for every 10 Model Ns they ordered. The little car accounted for most of the 8,828 units produced at Piquette Avenue in 1906.

Couzens, who not only strictly guided the company's finances but also directed advertising, had some Model N ads created to appeal to doctors. The copy suggested that a Model N "would enable them to visit three times as many patients daily as with a buggy," notes Nevins in *Ford: The Times, the Man, The Company*. But buyers flocked to the car for one main reason: It was a lot of car for the money.

The following year the Model N was joined by its close cousin, the slightly flashier Model R, which also became a sales leader.

Weighing 100 pounds more and costing $150 more than the N, the R flew out of Ford showrooms just as fast. It was built only as a 1907 model and was sold out by September, with 2,500 units having been produced. The same was true of the 1908 Model S, which paired with Model N production in 1908, and the two models combined for 6,398 sales that year.

While the Models N, R, and S were enjoying great success—and proving Ford's credo that buyers wanted lightweight, simple, inexpensive cars—Henry Ford was planning his next product move. Despite the popularity of his latest models, he had no plans to rest on his laurels.

During the winter of 1906–1907, he directed his most trusted employees—principally chief engineer Wills, machine tool expert Walter Flanders, design engineer Joseph Galamb, and recently hired Danish-born patternmaker and foundryman Charles Sorensen—to create a private work area on the third floor of the Piquette Avenue factory. Once partitions were framed up and doors fitted, access to the area would be limited to Ford's inner circle.

The project about to begin was top secret.

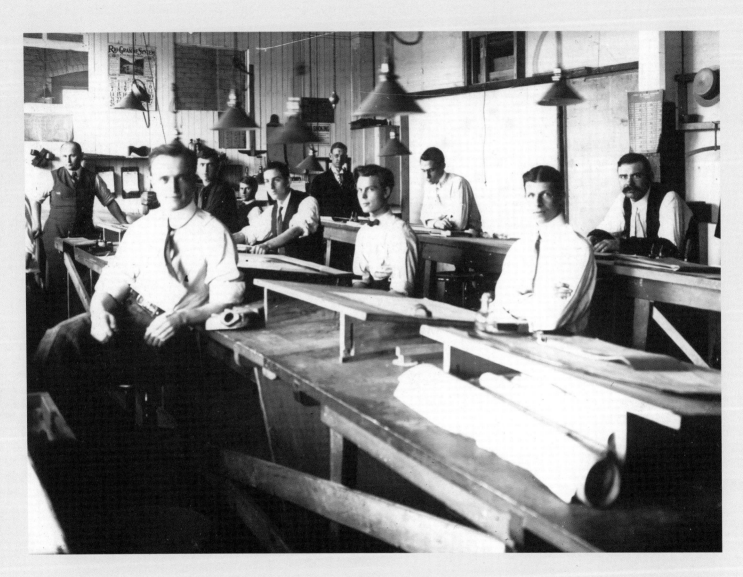

The drafting room in the Piquette Avenue plant during the early Model T era. Working at wooden tables under incandescent light and performing their calculations with slide rules, these draftsmen created the technical drawings used to make patterns, molds, and tooling for the car's approximately 5,000 parts. Today they'd be working at computer-aided design (CAD) terminals. *From the collections of The Henry Ford*

Chapter 2

THE MODEL T IS BORN

Genesis and mass production

The secret room on the third floor of the Piquette Avenue plant came together quickly in the gray cold of late 1906. In this small space, with its door just large enough to drive a car in and out, the development of what Henry Ford called "a completely new job"—the Model T—would take place. And although the area was fairly secluded, Ford had a lock fitted to the door to aid security.

"Mr. Ford did not want others in the plant to know anything about this [the T project] until it had been thoroughly worked out and, of course, he was perfectly right in this," recalled Charles Sorensen in *My Forty Years with Ford*.

The room was fitted with a lathe and a few basic shop tools. There was a comfortable rocking chair near the center of the room from which Ford would listen intently, offer ideas, encourage and guide his associates, and contemplate the progress.

But perhaps the most critical tools in the room were the four blackboards set up by Joe Galamb. These had proven indispensable during development of previous cars, since Ford, Wills, Galamb, and their assistants began each design by roughing it out in chalk—Henry Ford had difficulty comprehending standard mechanical drawings.

"A blueprint didn't mean much to him," noted Sorensen.

According to Sorensen, the blackboards used in Model T development served another purpose. The rough chalk drawings could be photographed to protect Ford against patent suits (the Selden battle was underway at the time). The photos, once they were officially dated, proved originality.

Development of the T's approximately 5,000 components proceeded swiftly, with the development team and Henry Ford often working until eight or nine o'clock at night. Galamb and his primary draftsmen, Gene Farkas and Charles Balough, converted the chalk renderings into fully dimensioned drawings using slide rules to do their engineering calculations. Working from the drawings, Sorensen's patternmakers then created full-scale wooden patterns, molds, and mockups that Henry Ford could examine, discuss with his team, and ultimately approve for prototype parts to be made.

"He wanted to see the finished size of the product; and that was where I came in," Sorensen recalled. "It was because of our constant tinkering that we were so right in many of the things we made. By whittling away at the wooden models of each part, and at the same time calculating the probable tensile strength of it in a few alloys of steel, we eventually came up with what was Model T."

When blueprints were ready, the parts were cast, machined, and assembled. Since the development team broke new technical ground in so many areas, they often found themselves wondering whether many of their innovations would work in the real world.

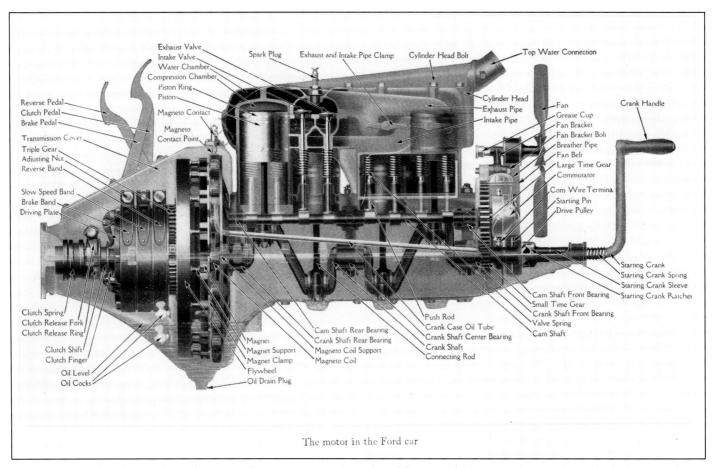

The motor in the Ford car

The early automakers frequently used cutaway illustrations to tout the technical features of their cars. This one shows the brilliant simplicity and overall robust design of Ford's four-banger. Note the compact flywheel magneto and two-speed planetary transmission. Today, these would be considered good examples of "systems engineering." *From the collections of The Henry Ford*

JOSEPH GALAMB
Chief body engineer

When Ford's chief engineer, C. Harold Wills, offered Joe Galamb a salary of $20 per week as a design draftsman at the Piquette Avenue plant in 1905, the Hungarian immigrant who had been living in the United States for only two years sensed a good opportunity. Galamb had been professionally trained at the Budapest Industrial Technology Engineering Course and had worked at auto companies in Germany and the United States before joining Ford. Almost immediately, he impressed Wills and Henry Ford with the quality and precision of his drawings.

After designing parts for the Models N and K, as well as prototype projects, Galamb was enlisted in Henry Ford's inner circle for the secret development of the Model T; the others were pattern-shop foreman Charles Sorensen and draftsmen Gene Farkas and Louis Halmesberger. Galamb served as the car's chief designer.

Historians have speculated why Wills, who had helped Henry Ford develop virtually every car since the company's founding, was not given a leading role in the Model T's core development team, although he contributed much to the car's metallurgy. Sorensen later wrote that "Mr. Ford didn't want Wills in on this work," without offering any explanation. Some veteran Ford observers and Model T buffs believe Henry remained stung from the underdeveloped Model K and its subsequent problems, and he may have blamed them on Wills.

Whatever the reason, Ford valued Galamb's talent to such a high degree that he gave him his own cubicle adjacent to the Experimental Department at Piquette. From there, Galamb churned out designs of the components and body structures that made up the Tin Lizzie.

Galamb succeeded Wills as the company's chief engineer in 1914. During the next three decades, his designs touched many innovative vehicles, including an army tank, the first Ford farm tractor, the chassis of the famous 1932 V-8 cars, and numerous vehicle body structures. Galamb retired from Ford in 1944.

Joseph Galamb

Henry's Brilliance

Henry Ford's intuitive gift for solving technical challenges (such as the size of gears required in the planetary gearbox) often amazed his colleagues. "He was quick to see precisely how an adjustment of parts could be bettered," Allan Nevins observed. "When a problem of thickness of materials, distribution of weight, or tensile strength arose, he sometimes solved it by sheer inspiration."

Ford's fertile mind contributed countless ideas. Joe Galamb and others credited Henry with the engine's cast-en-bloc cylinders (the basic concept originated in England), removable cylinder head, and flywheel magneto. Galamb was skeptical of the separate head, which was an industry first, because the gaskets of the day were not suitable to hold

against even the T's modest cylinder pressure. His fears proved unfounded.

The prototype crankshaft was another critical component that worried Ford, Galamb, and Sorensen when they first saw it. Ford's adoption of the new vanadium steels for many of the car's most highly stressed parts (approximately half of the 20 steel alloys in the Model T were vanadium grades) had allowed the initial forging to be extremely light and small.

"This didn't look quite right to us," commented Sorensen, "because we had much heavier cranks in our other engines." Yet when the finish-machined crankshaft was tested under twice the load it would ever endure in actual operation, it passed with flying colors.

Vanadium steel allowed Ford to reduce the size of the gears in its two-speed planetary transmission for the Model T compared with previous transmissions. This helped reduce the unit's overall size and allowed it to be fully enclosed. The transmission shared the engine's crankcase oil. This view shows (from left) the planetary gearset; the three bands controlling reverse, low gear, and high gear; the clutch; and the clutch spring. With the simple addition of a torque converter and hydraulic control, this unit would be functionally equivalent to a modern automatic transmission.
From the collections of The Henry Ford

This photograph, taken outside the Piquette Avenue plant in 1908, is thought to be of the prototype Model T. The car still wears the coat of dirt from Henry Ford's long-distance test drive from Detroit north to Iron Mountain, Michigan. *From the collections of The Henry Ford*

There were numerous technical detours and catastrophic failures along the T's development path. In a 1955 letter to Ford archivist Owen Bombard, published in the January 2007 edition of the Model T Ford Club International's excellent magazine, *Model T Times*, former draftsman Charles Balough recalled one incident concerning a prototype Model T. This particular car incorporated a sliding-gear, three-speed transmission in place of the regular Ford two-speed planetary gearbox. "Mr. Ford wasn't sold on this [sliding-gear] type but he was willing to give it a trial," wrote Balough.

In fact, Ford was dead set against anything other than his beloved (and simpler) planetary gearsets. Balough was assigned to conduct a trial of the car on public roads, as was done in the days before factory proving grounds. The road test began just before the dayshift left the plant.

All went well until a streetcar unexpectedly crossed Balough's path just as he was passing it. The collision crushed the prototype Model T and its experimental transmission between the streetcar and a telegraph pole. Balough escaped with a few bruises, but the T was demolished.

One of the first Model T advertisements from 1908 clearly shows the two-lever control setup that was combined with just two floor pedals on approximately the first 850–1,000 cars built in late 1908. After that, the arrangement was changed to the single lever and three pedals used through 1927. *From the collections of The Henry Ford*

The remains of the car were trucked back to the plant, and Balough feared Henry Ford's reaction to the mishap. Despondently, he told his friend Joe Galamb that he would look for another job, but Galamb convinced him to come to work the next morning at the usual time.

When Balough (whose weekly pay was $15) finally faced Ford and explained what happened, the boss broke out into a big smile and exclaimed, "Charlie, that's the best job you ever did for this company!"

According to Balough's letter, the accident ensured that a sliding-gear-type transmission would never be fitted to the Model T. Ford instructed Galamb and his designers to develop a new planetary with three forward speeds to replace the standard two-speed unit.

"We worked on this for several months only to establish that a three-speed transmission would involve the use of too many gears," he explained. Eventually an improved two-speed planetary was approved for the Model T.

The incident recalled a Henry Ford comment that became legendary among auto engineers: "The gear that gives you no trouble is the one that you never use." It typified Ford's belief in simplicity, which was manifest in the Model T.

Automotive electrical systems were often dismally unreliable in 1907, and Henry Ford knew that for his car to be successful it had to have a robust source of electricity for ignition spark and lighting. Integrating the car's magneto within the engine flywheel was Ford's solution, but the feat required long hours of tinkering by veteran Ford mechanic "Spider" Huff and others. Henry himself provided solutions, such as the encapsulation of the magneto's 16 separate electrical coils in a durable resin.

It cannot be overstated that the creation of the Model T was truly a team effort. In addition to the few key men profiled in many of this book's sidebars, many more provided invaluable brainpower and toil.

The car could not have been a success without George Holley's low-cost cast-iron carburetor. (Ford liked it so much he bought Holley's Detroit-based company, but later handed it back to Holley.) Nor could Model T have been so durable without John Wandersee who, along with Harold Wills, shepherded the application of the new vanadium steel alloys.

"John was an example of how in the early days we developed our own experts from our own people," recalled Sorensen in his book. Wandersee was a floor sweeper when he joined the Piquette Avenue plant; he had no engineering, chemical, or metallurgical experience. But Henry Ford immediately sensed his interest in technical subjects and soon gave him engineering projects.

"Mr. Ford wanted him because he felt he could rely upon any figures John brought him," Sorensen explained. "Wandersee was always able to come up with facts and not opinion." He eventually rose to be Ford's top metallurgist.

As noted by Allan Nevins in his almost biblical histories of the Ford Motor Company published in the 1950s, the sources of many of the Model T's innovations—the gear-driven fan, the carburetor mixture adjustment on the dashboard, the spark and throttle controls under the steering wheel, and the left-side steering column itself (to name a few)—will never be known. Some of the contributors certainly were inspired by the auto industry's technology boom in general, which was chronicled in period publications including *The Horseless Age* and its successor, *The Automobile*, *Motor Age*, as well as *The Engineer* and *Cycle and Automobile Trade Journal*.

Of course, while the T was introduced in October 1908, it actually had been in the works for more than four years—Ford's Models N, R, and S served as steppingstones to its development. But the overriding credit for "the car that put the world on wheels" unquestionably goes to Henry Ford, the clever, inquisitive, visionary machinist.

"His was the controlling plan for a light, powerful, trustworthy cheap car," asserted Nevins. "His was the guiding mind and his was clearly the most powerful personality."

Model T Lives!

When the last bolt had been torqued and some final adjustments made to a stuck transmission, the first of 15 million Model Ts emerged from its womb and was pushed toward the third-floor freight elevator. Once it was on the ground floor, a jubilant Ford and his team of confidants, accompanied by a growing throng of plant workers, marched the new machine into the sunlight.

A couple of gallons of gasoline were poured into the under-seat tank. Ignition on! Spark retarded! Sliding the throttle lever under the steering wheel a few degrees, Henry Ford signaled for the engine to be crank-started—a procedure that would sprain and even break countless arms and cause endless cursing for years, particularly in cold weather, until aftermarket electric starter kits became available and Ford offered its own electric starter.

Model T No. 1 sputtered into life and quickly settled into a steady idle, its mild exhaust note drowned out by the uproarious cheers from the crowd surrounding the car. Ford asked carburetor king George Holley to climb in next to him for the shakedown cruise into downtown Detroit, traversing the city's famous streets: Woodward Avenue, Michigan Avenue, and Lafayette.

Ford couldn't resist steering his new vehicle past Alexander Malcomson's coal distributorship in hopes that his former business partner, whose automotive vision was fixed on large, expensive, six-cylinder touring cars, would catch a glimpse of Henry's vastly different rolling revolution.

There was no question that the latest Ford was everything its designers knew it would be. While Ford began teasing the public with hints of his new car in March 1908, official production began in September. As author Nevins accurately

Ford made windshields, gas lamps, and tops standard equipment in 1909, the year this wintry photo of a new Runabout was taken outside the Piquette Avenue plant. Also called a Roadster, the Runabout sported a small, single-passenger rear seat, often dubbed a "mother-in-law seat." In the early years, the Model T bodies were made entirely of wood and built by outside suppliers: Wilson, Pontiac, and Hayes (later Kelsey-Hayes). *From the collections of The Henry Ford*

observed, "The wave of enthusiasm for the new model rolled across America and round the world."

Naturally, there were mechanical glitches with the early cars, some of them more acute than the teething variety.

The Spartan interior of a restored Runabout shows the single control lever at left and pedals embossed with the letters C (clutch), R (reverse), and B (brake). In early 1915, unmarked pedal surfaces replaced the lettered pedals. In the center is a Kingston ignition coil box; these items were wood through 1914 and steel thereafter. The speedometer is at right. *Artemis Images*

Rear-axle bearings were in soft Babbitt the first year, which caused many cars to require axle rebuilds until durable roller bearings were specified for 1910 production. The Model T's transmission bands were a weak point through most of the car's life, the cotton lining of the early bands being a shockingly fast-wearing material.

Model T owners' complaints (today known as "customer feedback") were somewhat nitpicky. The Touring model's original rear seat was a few inches too narrow for three passengers, but it was quickly widened to the public's satisfaction. Issues with certain parts flying off while in use were rectified with improved fasteners and rivets. Because the early T's front and rear wheels were of different sizes, owners were forced to strap on two sets of spare tires and inner tubes.

Henry Ford responded to some of the early issues by upgrading the troublesome parts, which helped set Model T's course as a remarkably reliable vehicle. "Service must be the best you can give," he wrote in *My Life and Work*, adding that parts interchangeability and standardized design allowed a Model T to remain on the road indefinitely.

However, once the Model T entered volume production, Ford's stated aim was to get the price down so that the customer would buy frequently.

"It is considered good manufacturing practice, and not bad ethics, occasionally to change designs," Ford noted, "so that old models will become obsolete and new ones will have to be bought either because repair parts for the old cannot be had, or because the new model offers a sales argument which can be used to persuade a consumer to scrap what he has and buy something new."

Super Factory—Highland Park

By 1908, Ford and Buick Motor Company were duking it out as makers of the most popular motor cars in the United States. Together with Reo (the initials of its founder, Ransom E. Olds)

and Maxwell-Briscoe, the four firms in 1908 sold more vehicles than all other U.S. automobile makers combined.

Ford was poised to assume the sales crown uncontested. Industry watchers agreed that moderately priced and sized cars were gaining popularity. "It was easy to acquire for $1,000 or less a better automobile than $3,000 would have bought in 1905," noted Nevins, the added value coming from rapid improvements in automotive technology. General efficiencies were rising, too, thanks to rapid advances in factory tools. Multi-spindle drills, for example, could simultaneously bore 45 holes in the side of an iron casting, saving hours of labor.

Ford's sprawling Highland Park super-factory showed the world how to mass-produce affordable, high-quality automobiles. The plant's power-generating plant with smokestacks is visible at center in this 1923 photograph. *From the collections of The Henry Ford*

When Ford moved into the new Highland Park plant in late 1909, the company had yet to implement its moving assembly line. These chassis awaiting their rear wheels in 1910 will be pushed to the next station, where their bodies will be installed. *From the collections of The Henry Ford*

Due to the success of the Model N, Ford had effectively outgrown the Piquette Avenue factory. With the advent of the Model T, a smash hit in its first year (General Motors president Billy Durant had even approached Henry Ford and James Couzens about selling their company, but was rebuffed), the top Ford Motor Company managers clearly recognized they needed a much larger plant.

What Ford had in mind was a super-factory. A few years earlier he had acquired a 60-acre tract just across Detroit's northern border in the suburb of Highland Park. It was there, on the grounds of a former racetrack bordering Woodward and Manchester avenues, that Ford built his entire manufacturing operation.

The huge complex would feature its own foundry, engine dynamometer building, and administration headquarters, all interconnected by a labyrinth of underground tunnels.

Inbound and outbound freight was handled by a network of feeder railway lines and loading docks. Inside the two four-story buildings linked by a vast central assembly shop, hundreds of miles of conveyor belts crisscrossed monorail trolleys and muscular overhead cranes, all with the ability to move great quantities of material expeditiously.

For the design of such an enormous compound, Ford went to Albert Kahn, a rising-star architect who, with his brother Julius, had designed a number of prominent industrial structures in Michigan, including the Packard Motor Car Company's main facility in Detroit. Kahn would go on to become perhaps the most famous industrial architect of the twentieth century.

Kahn's design was underpinned by reinforced concrete and steel to provide high strength and fire safety. He also favored extensive use of glass to maximize interior lighting

One of the most famous photographs in industrial history shows Ford's flywheel magneto line, which kicked off mass production at Highland Park in April 1913. The factory quickly became a melting pot of nationalities and ethnicities. By late 1914 more than 70 percent of the factory's 16,000 workers were foreign immigrants, many of whom spoke little or no English. *From the collections of The Henry Ford*

and plenty of rooftop ventilation. The more than 50,000 square feet of glazing, including hundreds of rooftop skylights, gave the plant its "Crystal Palace" nickname.

Kahn began work on the Highland Park plant in 1907, being careful to optimize the shop-floor layouts and workflow plan detailed by Ed Martin and Charles Sorensen. During late 1910, Ford moved into the largest, most modern automobile factory of the era. Highland Park was symbolized by its five mammoth smokestacks jutting skyward above the plant's

power house and the oversized letters F-O-R-D displayed between them. It was the primary home of Model T for its entire life, with the exceptions of late-1908 production at Piquette Avenue and engines built at the 1,100-acre River Rouge complex during the 1920s.

Mass Production Begins

Ford, Martin, and Sorensen first conceptualized a continuous-production system during the final months at Piquette

PETER E. MARTIN
Hard-driving production boss

P. E. Martin, known as Peter or Ed (his middle name was Edmund) within Ford Motor Company, was a machine operator in a Detroit tin-can factory when he was hired by Ford's chief engineer, C. Harold Wills, in early 1904. Like many of Ford's early factory men, Martin's lack of formal engineering training was offset by his natural understanding of machines and love of manufacturing, which helped land him his first job in the Experimental Department at Piquette Avenue.

"He had greater force of personality than his jowled face and placid, good-natured expression indicated," wrote Allan Nevins. Martin skyrocketed through the ranks. By fall of 1906, he was assistant manager of all of Ford's facilities, with Charles Sorensen reporting to him.

Before the Model T entered production in the fall of 1908, Martin and Sorensen completely reorganized the Piquette plant. They revised the shop-floor layout and prepared "operation sheets" detailing the work processes. They purchased new machines and carefully mapped out the operation of each. Martin also set up an inventory control department to regulate the flow of parts and stabilize production throughout the plant. Their system laid the groundwork for even greater efficiencies at Highland Park.

For most of his 38-year career at Ford, Martin was one of the few executives not affected by the dominating, somewhat ruthless Sorensen. Martin's personality and Sorensen's towering ego did not conflict when it came to the business of building cars.

"We had a sense of achievement by association, by teamwork," recalled Sorensen in his 1956 memoir.

While quiet and outwardly affable, Martin could drive his foremen and workers just as hard as the explosive Sorensen did, however.

"In the plant, just the sight of either man sent shivers through the average worker and was likely to be a subject for discussion at the workers' supper table that evening," noted Ford Bryan in *Henry's Lieutenants*. In some Ford histories, Martin is linked to the high workforce turnover prior to the five-dollar day, which he initially opposed.

But fate may have decreed that Ford's two top factory men would eventually butt heads, which happened in the 1920s. Martin tendered his resignation, but neither Henry nor Edsel would accept it. It would take a mild heart attack in the late 1930s to slow Martin, and he eventually retired in 1941.

Peter Martin

Mass production opened new opportunities for women to join America's industrial workforce. They were often given tedious jobs such as upholstery that required great dexterity, at the time thought to be a uniquely female attribute. Under Ford's original "five-dollar day" plan, only those women who were supporting families were eligible for the higher wages; unmarried women were not. *From the collections of The Henry Ford*

Avenue. They were inspired by the way machinist Walter Flanders had rearranged equipment to improve workflow in 1907. While the plant relied on trolleys and chain hoists to lift and move components, Ford installed a simple monorail for transporting parts in early 1908.

It was still commonplace then for manufacturing companies to arrange their tools and machinery according to type, for example, placing grinding machines in one area of the factory and drilling machines in another. Martin and

Sorensen instead began by installing the Ford equipment in the order in which it was needed in the manufacturing process. Grinders were placed next to drilling machines, which were set adjacent to brazing equipment. By forming a continuous production flow, Ford was able to greatly reduce the amount of work in the process and boost the speed of production.

The parts and components still had to be pushed and dragged from one operation to the next. Once the continuous-production process was proven in the manufacturing

Model T engines were tested in Highland Park's dynamometer department. These men had to be constantly on guard against fire, due to the unavoidable flammable vapors. The plant featured a full sprinkler system and other state-of-the-art defenses against fire. *From the collections of The Henry Ford*

operations, though, Ford's leaders applied the idea to assembly. Up until then, all vehicle assembly generally was done in one spot. The components were built up on benches, each man typically assigned to assemble one item at a time.

Martin and Sorensen decided instead to subdivide the assembly process into individual operations. For example, one worker would insert a bolt into a housing and then pass the housing to the next man, who fitted a washer and nut on the bolt. That man would then pass the work piece to the next worker, who would torque the bolt down, and so on.

Previously, it had taken 20 minutes per worker to assemble the Model T's unique flywheel magneto. By subdividing the labor, flywheel magneto assembly time was cut to only seven minutes per unit, with half as many workers needed.

Up to this point, the magneto assemblies were pushed from worker to worker along a smooth, metal-topped bench. In April 1913 (shortly after installation of the plant's first automatic conveyor, in the foundry), the magnetos were placed on a moving-chain system. This moved them from worker to worker at a set rate of speed that stabilized the

assembly process by slowing down the faster workers and speeding up the slower ones.

At first, Ford tried to run the line at 60 inches per minute, but that rate was found to be too fast and was reduced to 18 inches per minute, but that was too slow. Someone suggested a rate of 44 inches per minute, and it turned out to be perfect. As a result, magneto assembly time was cut to five minutes per unit, and the workforce on the line was reduced by 17 percent.

Experiments with a moving chassis assembly line took place even before it was tried on the magneto line. During Highland Park's slow period in summer 1913, Martin, Sorensen, and Clarence Avery (one of Edsel Ford's former teachers, who was hired for his brilliance in calculating production timing) had a heavy rope rigged to a chassis, which was then winched down the line. A group of six assemblers walked along with it, installing parts that were fetched by other workers.

This crude setup worked well, but the production bosses decided to place the parts alongside the line, with a

Within the mammoth Highland Park complex, Ford's continuous production flow resembled a series of rivers and tributaries. In this 1914 photo, brass radiators and fully assembled wheels stream from overhead and floor-level feeder lines to meet the chassis line. *From the collections of The Henry Ford*

worker assigned to each station to install a part as the car slowly passed by. This new arrangement was deemed a great success.

The concept spread to the engine and transmission assembly departments, where it was championed by foreman William Klann. The time to assemble the Model T's four-cylinder engine, which had been roughly 600 minutes of one man's time in fall 1913, had dropped to 226 minutes.

"Who would have thought in the old Piquette days, when a stationary knot of men put a motor together, that the division of that job into 84 different operations would enormously increase the speed of the shop?" asked Allan Nevins.

So by early fall 1913, just after the Dodge brothers had informed Henry Ford that they would stop supplying parts for the Model T within one year (and planned to produce their own car), Ford had successfully tested his moving assembly line for the three main elements of the car: engine, transmission, and chassis. In November, Ford production engineers put the entire engine assembly on an integrated

assembly line. The following spring, the process was put into production for chassis assembly, with the chassis guided by a simple track.

The effect on labor time, productivity, and required floor space was dramatic. When chassis were built up in one stationary spot, the process took 12 1/2 hours per chassis and consumed 6,000 feet of floor space. With the moving assembly line, the time was slashed to 1 1/2 hours per chassis and the process required only 300 feet of floor space.

Martin and Sorensen didn't waste time. If an employee offered a good idea, it wasn't studied to death. Encouraged by Ford, they immediately tried to determine how the idea could be incorporated into the production process, constantly refining the process at every chance. The automaker even switched to its immortal "any color as long as it's black" strategy in 1913. Recent scholarship indicates that this was because black paint was cheaper and more durable than other colors, not because black paints at the time dried much faster, as has been widely suggested in the past.

CHARLES SORENSEN
From patternmaker to production mastermind

Few at Ford could match Charles Sorensen in stamina, quick thinking, and organizational prowess. Perhaps fewer still had his high ambition, grenade-like temper, and dedication to the company. He was a leader, but he could be cutthroat to those who crossed him. Together, these qualities made the tall, commanding Dane one of Henry Ford's greatest assets during the birth and subsequent success of the Model T.

Sorensen came to Ford in 1905 from Detroit's thriving iron-stove industry, where as an apprentice patternmaker he learned drafting, basic metallurgy, tool design, and machining techniques. With experience gained in the stove foundries, he started as an assistant patternmaker, earning $3 per day. Henry Ford frequented the pattern shop, since he preferred to study a physical part rather than decipher blueprints, which was not one of his proficiencies. As a result, Ford and Sorensen spent much time together sharing their knowledge, and Sorensen learned of Ford's vision to build an affordable, durable car for the masses.

Ford promoted Sorensen to assistant production superintendent under Peter Martin (whom Sorensen called Ed) while also keeping him as the pattern department foreman. At the time of Model N development, all cylinder-block castings were made from hardwood patterns reinforced with brass. The wooden patterns lacked the durability needed for the high-volume production Henry Ford envisioned.

He came up with the idea of making metal rather than wooden patterns, which resulted in higher-quality, lower-cost castings. Sorensen worked quickly. He

Charles Sorensen

often was able to convert Ford's ideas into useful patterns and molds before drawings could be produced. His affinity for using iron castings earned him the nickname "Cast-Iron Charlie," which stuck with him for the rest of his career.

Casting techniques developed by Sorensen for the Model N inspired Henry Ford to produce the Model T's cylinder block and cylinders as a single unit—known as en-bloc casting—and enabled the use of a removable cylinder head. The en-bloc design greatly increased productivity, saved cost, and improved engine quality. Both en-bloc casting and the separate head became industry standards and were used on Sorensen's casting masterpiece, the 1932 flathead V-8.

The long list of Sorensen's accomplishments at Ford includes implementing the Keim Mills parts-making acquisition in 1911, assisting in the adoption of new vanadium-steel alloys, participating in the design of the first Ford farm tractors, and managing worldwide tractor production. When the U.S. tractor-making operation moved to the new River Rouge complex after World War I, Sorensen built a czar-like reputation at the mega-plant. Later, his harsh treatment of Ford dealers and ongoing political infighting alienated him from a number of Ford managers, including Edsel.

Still, Cast-Iron Charlie's greatest achievement was in the early 1940s, when he directed Ford's tooling and high-volume production of radial aircraft engines and the construction of the gigantic Willow Run factory, which at its peak produced one B-24 heavy bomber per hour.

Each completed chassis ended up at this "rolling road" station, where the entire powertrain was tested for the first time. The worker at left has filled the T's cooling system while his colleague sits on the gas tank, applies full throttle, and listens for any worrisome sounds amid the din. *From the collections of The Henry Ford*

Continuous production and the moving assembly line seemed to spread organically within Ford's factory. Feeder lines running overhead, under the floor, and every which way became like tributaries to a river, with the brooks and streams carrying every conceivable part toward the main waterway (assembly).

The system, with its ballet-like choreography and continuous motion, amazed even those employed there. By 1922, amid Ford's ramp-up to the astounding 2.2 million–unit record-production year, Henry Ford described in *My Life and Work* the further improved operation this way:

Every piece of work in the shop moves; it may move on hooks on overhead chains going to assembly in the exact order in which the parts are required; it may travel on a moving platform, or it may go by gravity. But the point is that there is no lifting or trucking of anything other than materials.

Critics of Ford and of twentieth-century industry in general claimed that mass production took the skill out of work. Certainly it was true that the era of hand-built automobiles made by "Old World craftsmen" who spent hours

By late summer 1913, Highland Park was producing more than 3,000 Model Ts per day on three shifts. Ford's production process increased annual output from 75,000 to 300,000 units, as the time required to make each car fell from 12 1/2 hours to 83 minutes. This photo taken in August 1913 shows the 1,000 chassis built in a single shift. *From the collections of The Henry Ford*

grinding, filing, and test-fitting parts before assembly could no longer compete for mainstream markets against Ford's high-volume enterprise.

In his memoir, Sorensen argued that "by putting higher skill into planning, management, and tool building it is possible for skill to be enjoyed by the many who are not skilled." He correctly noted that a million men working with their hands could never equal the daily output of the Ford assembly line.

Ford continued to refine the subdivision of assembly. With time-and-motion studies, workers' movements were observed to find new ways to reduce waste. While it has been suggested that Henry Ford relied on Frederick Taylor's principles of scientific management, evidence indicates that Ford developed his time-and-motion studies independently. Additionally, Taylor's principles involved much more than just time and motion. Of course, Ford didn't have a lock on new and better factory methods; Buick, Cadillac, Reo, White, and a few others brought innovations, too. But executives and engineers who visited Highland Park from auto companies all over the world, and from other industries, had never seen a manufacturing system so bold, comprehensive, and efficient as that of the Ford Motor Company.

Touring bodies receive their final varnish coat in the Highland Park paint shop in 1915. Skilled workers apply the clear varnish using applicators comprising several small nozzles fed by low-pressure hoses. The varnish was flowed on horizontally and the excess ran off the body into catch trays that returned it to the varnish tanks. The wet varnish had a molasses-like consistency and took approximately one week to dry in a warm, dry storage area (some Model T metal parts were coated with japan, which dried faster than varnish). Ford adopted its famous "any color as long as it's black" strategy in 1914 because black was cheaper and more durable than other colors. The company couldn't switch its body line to the enamels that appeared around 1915 because the paint required high-temperature curing ovens that would damage or burn the T's wooden body framing. Note, also, the cars' fully upholstered interiors. *From the collections of The Henry Ford*

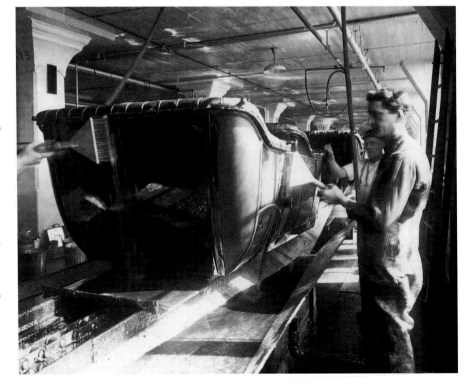

Above: Touring bodies have their tops installed in 1914, a process that required a considerable amount of hand-fitting. During this period at Highland Park, 148 women and 12 men worked in the plant's Top Department, turning out approximately 700 tops for all Model T variants in each eight-hour shift. *From the collections of The Henry Ford*

Left: The blockbuster success of the Model T, the five-dollar day, and other innovations made Henry Ford the most publicly scrutinized industrialist of the early twentieth century. In many ways, he was indeed the magician depicted in this 1920 editorial cartoon. *From the collections of The Henry Ford*

The proof of the manufacturing system was in the show-room. Once Ford reduced the price of its basic Model T Runabout first to $550, then to $500, it opened a price gap of nearly $450 between the T and the next best low-priced car. By July 1914, Ford announced the Runabout's price had been further dropped to $440, delighting Ford's 7,000 U.S. dealers.

President Woodrow Wilson purchased a Model T for his summer home. Ford opened a sales agency in Iceland. And at Highland Park, a new Model T was leaving the final assembly line every 60 seconds or less.

Tin Lizzie's Demise

When World War I ended in 1918 (Ford had produced ambulance chassis, steel helmets, and Liberty V-12 aero-engine cylinders for the effort), Henry Ford expected his company to return to its prewar market dominance based exclusively on the Model T. But while output doubled from 1918 to 1919, it plummeted the following year.

The United States fell into a recession in 1920. Lincoln, Willys-Overland, and GM were in financial trouble. Ford had spent heavily, and cash reserves were low. He had bought out the Dodge brothers' shares, and his colossal Rouge mega-factory in Dearborn that dwarfed Highland Park was still under construction. Additionally, he had purchased hundreds of thousands of acres of timberland in northern Michigan, plus coal and ore mines for the purpose of making Ford Motor Company a completely vertically integrated enterprise.

The weak economy caused Model T sales to nosedive, prompting Ford to slash prices below cost and force unwanted cars on dealers. The situation turned worse, as the company for the first time in many years could not pay its bills. Bankruptcy loomed.

Averse to loans, Henry Ford decided to shut down his plants for five weeks, from December 23 through February 1. Various surplus equipment was auctioned off in an attempt to raise cash, and 58,000 Highland Park and Rouge plant workers were put in limbo without pay.

During this tense period a number of salaried employees were fired or resigned, including many of Ford's old associates who had helped launch the Model T and build the legend. These included veteran chief engineer C. Harold Wills, treasurer Frank Klingensmith, sales manager Norval Hawkins, and William Knudsen, who went on to lead Chevrolet into the number-one sales spot.

Ford's tight purse strings helped the company weather the storm through 1921, when the national economy rebounded: the Roaring Twenties had begun! Model T production nearly doubled again to over one million units. The T still had no peer, despite attempts by competitors to assault the king of the low-priced car segment.

After setting its stupendous 2.2 million production record in 1923, Ford's output of Model Ts remained strong and steady, at slightly more than 2 million units annually (nearly 10,000 cars per day) in 1924–1925. Such volume gave Ford more than 50 percent of the U.S. car market. By every measure, the Model T was still a phenomenal success, but behind the bright numbers Ford's situation was becoming dark indeed.

Despite his refusal to consider a new car to replace the T, Henry Ford in the early 1920s directed the Experimental Department to begin development of a family of engines with a radical X configuration. The layout of an X-8 resembled two V-4s with a common crankshaft. Prototypes were built using various valvetrains and cooling systems, but the X layout caused lubrication and induction problems. The project was abandoned in 1926, but Ford ultimately triumphed with the 1932 V-8. *From the collections of The Henry Ford*

Why would a woman in dress attire be standing in the Highland Park plant, watching cars roll off the assembly line? To convey that sophisticated women longed for a 1925 Model T Coupe, that's why. By the mid-1920s, the T was in decline, Chevrolet was on the rise in the low-priced car segment, and Ford had only the mildly facelifted 1926 T in the works. For the Tin Lizzie, the end was approaching. *From the collections of The Henry Ford*

The fundamental reason was simple: The Model T had lived way past its prime, remaining virtually unchanged from its 1909 introduction (see Chapter 3). "I was sick of looking at them," noted Charles Sorensen.

By the 1920s, America and its automobiles had changed greatly since the days of Piquette Avenue. Improved roads over longer distances required more power and better brakes than the T's measly 22 horses and pathetic binders could muster. Electric starters, demountable wheel rims, and a smoother ride were now expected on all cars, and improvements in transmission and clutch design had made shifting via gear lever the preferred engineering choice. Style and color also had become purchase factors.

Because of these changes, the style-less, gloomy-black, old-tech T was threatened by an emboldened Chevrolet's new Superior K and Superior V models. The 1925 Chevys offered far more value per dollar than the Model T, despite their higher prices. To make matters worse, GM chairman Alfred Sloan instituted the annual model change, which was the antithesis of Henry Ford's dogma.

Based on rapidly improving cars with greater pizzazz, and the expertise of new boss William Knudsen, Chevrolet

WILLIAM KNUDSEN
Factory genius who later haunted Ford

A tall, lanky Dane who didn't shy away from a fight, Bill Knudsen came to Ford when the automaker purchased the John R. Keim Mills (where he was an employee) in Buffalo, New York, in 1911. Knudsen was a fast learner regarding the latest production methods and had helped Keim switch from bicycle manufacturing to producing various stamped-metal components—drive axle housings, fuel tanks, fenders, and mufflers—for the Model T. Henry Ford wanted Knudsen to apply his expertise and tremendous energy for making vehicles to his role as plant superintendent.

Knudsen "remained ready for any task, however dirty," wrote Ford historian Allan Nevins, including overseeing the transfer of Keim's tooling and 62 employees to Highland Park in 1912. This gave Ford the capability to produce its own stamped parts in-house. The ex-Keim Buffalo facility was converted into a Ford vehicle plant after Knudsen demonstrated the complete teardown and perfect reassembly of a Model T.

Knudsen was in his element in a factory. He seemed to have a sixth sense in arranging tooling and machines to give the most efficient production flow. Soon after joining Ford, he was assigned to the company's expansion program, directing the opening of assembly plants in 30 U.S. locations. Working with legendary architect Albert Kahn, Knudsen focused on developing the production layout first, then creating the best building structure to support it, which was counter to the way factories had been constructed previously.

As Highland Park's manufacturing boss during World War I, Knudsen oversaw army truck, ambulance, and Liberty aero-engine production, as well as Ford's Eagle Boat submarine chasers built in a special yard on the Rouge River in Dearborn. But a heated altercation with Charles Sorensen in 1918 began a

William Knudsen

political battle between the two men that lasted until Knudsen resigned from Ford three years later.

Unfortunately for the Ford Motor Company, its loss was General Motors' gain. Knudsen joined GM in 1922 as vice president and quickly was made general manager of the struggling Chevrolet division. By 1931, Chevy production had eclipsed that of Ford, due in large part to greater efficiencies instituted by the vigorous Knudsen. During World War II, he was commissioned U.S. Army lieutenant general in charge of military production. Knudsen returned to GM after the war.

Ford Touring Car $295

F. O. B. DETROIT
Starter and Demountable Rims $85 Extra

OF all the times of the year when you need a Ford car, that time is NOW!

Wherever you live—in town or country—owning a Ford car helps you to get the most out of life.

Every day without a Ford means lost hours of healthy motoring pleasure.

The Ford gives you unlimited chance to get away into new surroundings every day—a picnic supper or a cool spin in the evening to enjoy the countryside or a visit with friends.

These advantages make for greater enjoyment of life—bring you rest and relaxation at a cost so low that it will surprise you.

By stimulating good health and efficiency, owning a Ford increases your earning power.

Buy your Ford now or start weekly payments on it.

Ford discontinued all paid advertising from 1917 to 1922, but then kicked back in with multimillion-dollar ad spending from 1923 through early 1926. The aim, in conjunction with hefty price reductions, was to boost the Model T's sagging sales and bolster the company's image, which suffered as Henry Ford's autocratic power came under fire in the press. *From the collections of The Henry Ford*

production rose steadily through the 1920s. And while twice as many (1.55 million) of the modestly revamped Model Ts as Chevrolets (692,000) were sold in 1926, the ratio two years before had been six to one. But Henry Ford remained blinded by his car's success.

"He fervently believed that if changes were made to his beloved creation, his formula for success would vanish," observed author Henry Dominquez in his fascinating book, *Edsel: The Story of Henry Ford's Forgotten Son*.

Ford's ire had been infamously raised in 1912 when, returning to Highland Park after a trip to Europe, he was surprised by a stylish T-based prototype that had been parked in an office area for his review. The shiny red four-door was longer than a production Model T, and its body and chassis were mounted lower to the ground. Today, this would

be called a design proposal, built for executive review. Chief engineer Harold Wills and his designers who created the car were anxious for the boss's reaction.

With little delay, Henry Ford attacked the poor prototype. He kicked, pounded, and ripped it wildly, "knocking it to pieces" as the stunned Wills and his colleagues watched, according to Allan Nevins. End of discussion.

Ford's resolve seemed to harden as the voices from his dealers (many of whom were switching to GM) asking for new products grew louder. Nor would he listen to his 33-year-old son, Edsel, who had grown up in the company and had been Ford's president for nearly eight years.

Edsel received a humiliating browbeating from his father when, in the Highland Park executive dining room, he suggested that Ford adopt hydraulic brakes like other automakers.

ERNEST KANZLER
Fired for talking straight

An attorney by education, and the brother-in-law of Edsel Ford, Ernest Kanzler was hired in 1916 by Henry Ford to manage logistics at the Henry Ford and Son tractor factory in Dearborn. During the next four years, he created a system that closely linked the arrival of inbound parts with tractor assembly and shipment of finished product. Kanzler's system, which was a preview of the just-in-time production methods used today, kept inventories low and helped speed delivery of new tractors to dealers, saving the company millions in the process.

When Kanzler was transferred to Highland Park in 1920, he applied the same processes to Model T production. Keeping the sales pipeline filled and dramatically reducing inventories enabled Ford to pay for materials virtually while the company was being paid by its dealers—the ideal 60- to 90-day transaction cycle.

Kanzler was at the helm of production scheduling when Model T output reached its zenith: 1.05 million cars in 1921 (the first million-unit year), rising to the record 2.2 million units in 1923, and continuing at well over a million cars annually through 1926. To keep the customers coming he instituted, with Henry's reluctant support, a weekly payment plan and a dealer-financed national advertising campaign.

However, Ernest Kanzler's finest moment was actually the six-page letter he sent to Henry Ford in January 1926. Written with eloquence and diplomacy, the memo intended to bring the incendiary issue of a Model T successor, and Ford's future beyond the T in general, directly to the founder. The topic of replacing the T had become urgent throughout the Ford enterprise—from dealers forced to sell an increasingly obsolete product, to the company's top executives who feared Henry Ford's reaction to replacing the 17-year-old flivver. Finally, Kanzler took the heroic step.

"I do not think the Model T will continue to be a satisfactory product to maintain our position in the automobile field," his memo stated, explaining that "competitors had made great strides" while Ford was losing customers. Kanzler praised the boss for his interest in the novel X-Engine project, but he noted that "there should also be other development in process of a power unit along conventional lines," proposing an inline six (a configuration Ford hated).

He received no reply from Henry Ford, and for the next eight months he was treated as persona non grata by the founder at every meeting. He was eventually fired in August 1926.

Ernest Kanzler

After Henry Ford in 1926 reluctantly accepted the need to design a successor to the Model T, the project moved ahead with conviction. Edsel Ford styled the handsome Model A, seen here, and a core team of Model T veterans—Joe Galamb, Gene Farkas, Charlie Sorensen, and Peter Martin—led the car's engineering and development. Henry, of course, was involved in every key decision. But Ford's plants were geared strictly for Model T production; converting them to build the 1928 Model A took six long months, costing Ford the industry's sales leadership. *From the collections of The Henry Ford*

Henry became enraged; he would not have pressurized, fluid brakes on his cars. In another losing battle with the founder, production manager Ernest Kanzler got the sack after sending Henry a six-page memo in which he reasoned that Ford needed to develop a six-cylinder T replacement quickly.

"As a single-purpose man, he could not abandon the biggest single purpose of his life," stated Sorensen in *My Forty Years with Ford*. "That achievement brought him worldwide renown which he enjoyed to the fullest. Vanity alone would keep him from acknowledging that Model T was outdated."

Without advanced vehicle development programs ready to meet the new market realities, Ford found itself up against the wall by the start of 1927. Then, halfway through the year, Henry Ford did what many hoped for but few believed would ever happen. On May 26, he ordered all Model T production stopped. Highland Park and 30 other plants fell silent, putting more than 60,000 workers in Detroit alone out of work.

The much-improved and genuinely handsome Model A would not appear for another six months. The long layoff allowed Henry Ford to build considerable suspense with the public for the next new Ford. It was definitely one of the toughest acts to follow in automotive history, but anyone who doubted the stubborn automaker's talent for delivering another great car was proven wrong.

Long before minivans and sport-utility vehicles, the Ford four-door sedan was the family-hauler of choice. This 1923 model posing with mom and sons wears a neat set of solid disc wheels, a type available on the aftermarket. On the unpaved rural roads that were common in 1920s America, these wheels offered much greater strength and durability than the wooden-spoked wheels. *From the collections of The Henry Ford*

Chapter 3

TIN LIZZIE EVOLVES

Charting the changes of the "changeless" Model T

The belief that Model T was "never changed" during its groundbreaking 18-year production run (19 years if you count the 308 cars assembled in fourth quarter 1908) must be one of the greatest automotive myths ever perpetuated—along with the notion that every T made was painted black!

Certainly the Tin Lizzie was not re-engineered or profoundly altered after the basic design was stabilized in early 1909 (after the initial 2,500 cars had been built). Even after the moderate restyling in the final 1926–1927 model years, the car was essentially the same old flivver that it had been two decades earlier.

During its long lifespan, however, the T was given literally thousands of subtle upgrades and modifications for the purposes of increasing durability, rectifying problems encountered in service, increasing factory productivity, cutting costs, and, in some minor cases, boosting the car's sales appeal.

Every cent that Ford saved in components and materials helped reduce the car's retail price to the "you'd be crazy not to buy one" level. An example of a specification that was directly influenced by Ford's cost-reduction mantra was the move away from the T's full-leather upholstery that was standard from 1909 to 1912. In 1913 came "leatherette" (synthetic faux leather) inner door panels. Leatherette back cushions followed in 1914 and, in 1915–1916, all-leatherette with "real" leather patches at the doors only. In late 1916, the last hint of genuine animal hide in the Model T was displaced by stamped-steel door covers.

One of Ford's earliest Model T advertisements shows a "two-lever" Touring, one of the initial batch of approximately 850–1,000 cars built with the reverse lever and two floor pedals. *From the collections of The Henry Ford*

The early control arrangement with reverse lever, as seen on The Henry Ford's 1909 Touring. This arrangement was superseded by the single-lever setup with reverse-gear pedal that entered production in February. *Author photo*

The first lesson for Model T hobbyists or anyone simply interested in the vehicle is: Beware of generalizations! Two cars produced in the same model year could differ in numerous ways. One reason for this is that the same part sourced from two different suppliers might be slightly different.

Another reason is that Ford simply altered the component in production, as sometimes occurred with stamped sheet metal, to tweak the car's appearance or provide a practical improvement. For example, steel hoods gave way to aluminum during 1909 production; both plain and louvered hoods were used on 1915 models (the latter offering better cooling); and plain and lipped front fenders were both fitted on pre-1917 cars.

The second lesson is that changes usually were phased in over a period of time, rather than instituted on an exact date, according to Model T expert Bruce McCalley, whose superb books, *Model T Ford* and *From Here to Obscurity* (the latter written with fellow T guru Ray Miller), are absolutely essential to understanding the car's ongoing development and technical history.

While it is commonly held that the first 2,500 Model Ts were equipped with gear-driven centrifugal water pumps, McCalley notes that some water-pump engines were built simultaneously with the newer types. Thus, the first thermo-siphon engine (sans water pump) was No. 2448, not No. 2500, and the second was No. 2455.

The water-pump engines also had slightly shorter cylinder blocks and crankshafts, and very small ignition timers (commutators). These and other features meant that the later-style factory parts (except pistons, connecting rods, and the oil pan/transmission cover) were not interchangeable with the earlier items.

Finally, the third lesson for Model T hobbyists is to consult experts in the Model T clubs and parts vendors, along with technical reference publications and restoration

Though it resembled a telephone booth on wheels, the 1909 Coupe offered closed-car weather protection for $950. This model was produced through 1911; early Coupe bodies were made by C. R. Wilson. The first approximately 2,500 Ts built through mid-April 1909 were fitted with centrifugal water pumps. Coupe bodies, fenders, aprons, frame, and running gear were painted a very dark green. This factory illustration is typical of the era's product images. *From the collections of The Henry Ford*

guides, many of which are listed under Resources in this book's appendixes. You cannot have too much information on any subject in the old-car hobby or in automotive history in general, and that rule definitely applies to Ford's Model T.

Some Commonalities

As noted in the Introduction, the Model Ts produced at Piquette Avenue prior to mid-April 1909 (up to approximately serial number 2500) differed dramatically from those that came after, to such a degree that Ford regularly referred to the early units as "the 1909 Fords under number 2500."

The rarest of this ultra-rare batch of Ts, estimated to be the first 850 to 1,000 cars, featured two control pedals and two floor-mounted levers. Because Henry Ford did not like this setup, he had Joe Galamb redesign it to include a third pedal (reverse gear) between the first two. This was the end of the hand-lever-actuated reverse gear. Galamb also modified the brake lever.

Production of the new three-pedal cars commenced in late February 1909, and Ford was so committed to the improvement that the company offered a kit ($15) to convert the two-pedal cars to the new design. Purchase of the kit

required that the owner return all of the parts in the original system to the factory.

As the Model T evolved over the years, it also lost some of its original pep. The 1909–1911 engines boasted the highest compression ratio—a heady 4.5:1—which, along with 60-psi cylinder compression, were major factors in the powerplant's claimed 22-horsepower output. But as the quality and energy content of U.S. gasoline was inconsistent at best from the late teens through most of the 1920s, Ford progressively reduced the T's compression ratio to suit this, first in 1912, then again in 1915. In addition, the introduction of features that enhanced passenger comfort, like fully enclosed bodies, increased the cars' weight.

In 1917, Ford fixed the T's standard compression ratio at 3.98:1, with 45-psi cylinder compression (a level that today might be associated with the simplest air-cooled industrial engines). This spec continued to the end of production and, according to T experts, the 1917–1927 engine provided 20 horsepower.

With a few notable exceptions, the early Model T wooden bodies gave way to metal exterior panels (mostly steel, but in some cases aluminum to save weight) over a

Antique Ford and Lincoln collector John Forster has owned this outstanding 1909 Touring for 20 years. When he purchased the car it wore Ford Grey but still had its original Carmine Red underneath. In 2001, Forster entrusted Leonard Davis of Waterford, Michigan, with the car's full restoration. The results speak for themselves. *Jim Frenak/FPI Studios*

hardwood frame. Some 1909 Touring models, including this book's cover car, had Pontiac sheet-aluminum bodies.

Interestingly, the 1913 Touring was the first Ford to feature front doors designed in the bodies. And strangely, the left front (driver's) door was a non-operational dummy and remained that way (except in Canadian-built Fords) until 1926! In 1912, a Fore-Door version of the Touring appeared with factory-fitted front door units; these were actually removable and could be purchased as parts to retrofit 1911–1912 Touring cars already on the road.

All radiators of the Model T "brass era," ending September 1916, were dimensionally identical but differed in that approximately the first 2,500 had a leading and trailing stroke (often called "wings") on the Ford script embossed into the radiator tank. A few of these, however, bore no name at all. The later brass radiators displayed the Ford script in its now-iconic form.

The winged script and the block-lettered Ford hubcaps were actually carried over from the 1908 Model S. The V-shaped radiators sometimes seen were not genuine Ford

The pristine cockpit of John Forster's 1909 Touring shows the car's operational essentials (from left to right): hand-brake lever (which also engages neutral); ignition advance lever, on the left side of the steering column; throttle lever, on the right side of the column; the clutch, reverse, and brake pedals; Kingston ignition coil box; carburetor enrichening knob; and speedometer. The silver badge mounted to the dashboard above the speedo is a 1909 Michigan state vehicle registration medallion, numbered 10011. *Jim Frenak/FPI Studios*

parts, and neither were the literally thousands of accessory items offered by a booming aftermarket created to serve and, in many cases, improve the Model T. One of the most popular add-ons was the Kales-Haskel Company's Hind-View Auto Reflector, which was first sold exclusively for Fords in August 1911, just three months after race driver Ray Harroun introduced the first rearview mirror on his Marmon-Wasp at the Indianapolis 500.

The 1914-style Ford, while similar to the 1913 except for door shape, was the last with the truly vintage appearance created by its straight fenders, acetylene gas lamps, and bicycle-tech bulb horn.

At this point it is worth noting that Henry Ford's eternally famous comment on the Model T's livery—"the customer can have any color he wants, as long as it is black"—was made in 1913 after the company had adopted black lacquer paint for its lower cost and durability. The lasting impact of Ford's quote has misled everyone but Model T hobbyists and students of Ford history, who know that the 1909–1913 cars,

continued on page 83

Above: The Stewart Model 11 brass speedometer with odometer and tripmeter was a $25 option on 1909 Fords. Its 60-mile-per-hour calibration was optimistic by perhaps 15 miles per hour, at least on a flat road. Speedos made by Jones, National, Johns-Manville, Sears Cross, Standard, AC, and other suppliers were also available on Fords through 1927. *Jim Frenak/FPI Sudios*

Right: In researching the history of his '09 Touring, John Forster found that the car had fallen derelict by the early 1930s. It was fully rebuilt by a Ford dealer who wanted to keep his mechanics employed during the Depression. The car's body, featuring aluminum panels, was made by the Pontiac Body Company, one of Ford's suppliers. The step surface of the early wooden running boards was linoleum. *Jim Frenak/FPI Studios*

Left: Until welded steel body structures began entering the auto industry in the early 1920s, hardwood frames were the common method of construction. A Model T was basically cabinetry underneath the stamped-steel or, in the case of early Tourings, aluminum exterior panels. This 1925 Tudor body framework hangs from the ceiling of The Henry Ford Museum. Though relatively heavy, this would not be considered a rigid structure today. *Author photo*

Below: They aren't known as "brass era" cars for nothing! The 1909–1910 models had the early "winged" version of the Ford script stamped into their radiator shells, which were made by Briscoe, McCord, or the Detroit Radiator Company, depending on production date. Post-1910 radiators were made by Ford. Other details worth noting include the speedometer drive gear on the right-front wheel, the transverse leaf spring front suspension, and the neat leather holster for the engine crank. *Jim Frenak/FPI Studios*

The 1909 Ford's Edmund & Jones (E&J) model 466 headlamps were powered by a carbide-acetylene gas generator. Other early-Ford headlamps were sourced from Brown and Atwood Castle. *Jim Frenak/FPI Studios*

continued from page 79
as well as the final 1926–1927 models, were available in a range of colors.

The transitional Model T of 1915 attempted to push into a more-modern form. The year's portfolio included two enclosed body types: the so-called Centerdoor Sedan with two central side doors and the Coupelet, Ford's first convertible coupe. The open-body types continued unchanged until April 1915.

The new-style cars featured magneto-powered electric headlamps, straight front and curved rear fenders, a louvered hood (though, as mentioned earlier, some 1915 hood stampings were unlouvered), a stamped-steel cowl fairing out to the body and mounting an unbraced windshield, and a Klaxon horn.

A "new look" came to the T in 1917. Front and rear fenders were curved and crowned. The hood was enlarged, tapering gently from the higher, slicker (and less costly to make) stamped-steel radiator shell right up to the sharply curved cowl. This relatively big step forward in Model T styling set the pace for most of the next decade.

Unchanged in size or appearance, the T gained two major mechanical improvements in 1919: an optional electric starter and demountable wheel rims.

The year 1923 brought refinements of line and trim in the form of a lowered body, a more easily deployed "one-man" top, and a four-door sedan.

Then, in a belated attempt to inject up-to-date style—and a return to colors!—the 1926–1927 cars enjoyed major aesthetic upgrades. But the old Lizzie had reached the end of its development, and in June 1927 the assembly lines that had cranked out cars more prodigiously than any other automaker were shut down. Ford continued to warehouse Model T parts, but soon after, the vastly superior Model A was launched in 1928, and the T's 1908 tooling and molds were discarded or scrapped.

AaaOOOgah! More elegant antique-brass hardware for John Forster to polish includes the Rubes bulb horn and E&J "Patent 1908" gas side lamps. *Jim Frenak/FPI Studios*

Tracking the T Year by Year

To provide a bit more granularity to the evolution of Mr. Ford's baby, the following section chronicles the Model T's changes on a year-by-year basis. It does not pretend to be a restoration guide (there are expert sources for that; see appendixes), but rather a novice's road map through the car's remarkable 19-year life.

1909

The brand-new Ford Model T was officially launched to the public in October 1908.

Today, 2.9 liters is considered large displacement for a four-cylinder engine, but in the T the 22-horsepower flathead looked small under the hood. The 1909 unit inhales through a Kingston carburetor and features Ford's thermo-siphon cooling. Note the ceramic-insulated ignition-coil posts protruding through the wooden firewall. *Jim Frenak/FPI Studios*

Body Types and Prices

Touring	Runabout	Coupe	Town	Tourster
$850	$825	$950	$1,000	—

Noteworthy Features: Winged Ford logo on brass radiator tank; one-piece oil pan; flat, rectangular door on transmission cover; open valve chambers in cylinder block.

First 1,000 Cars (through late February 1909): Low, flat 15-bolt cylinder head without Ford script. Two-pedal/two-lever control system.

First 2,500 Cars (through mid-April 1909): Gear-driven water pump with fan on end of pump shaft. Cylinder block without front coolant jacket. Wooden running boards covered with linoleum. Steel hood. Three-pedal control system adopted. Carburetors mainly Kingston, but some Buffalo carbs also used.

Cars After No. 2500 (late April 1909 onward): Thermo-siphon cooling system replaced water pump. Leather-belt-driven fan. New cylinder-head casting included enlarged coolant passages and frontal dome with the name "Ford Motor Co." in block letters embossed on top of head. New cylinder block with coolant jacket extending around front cylinder. Stamped-steel running boards with longitudinal ribs. Aluminum hood. Bodies constructed mainly of wood, but some Pontiac bodies built with sheet-aluminum panels over a hardwood frame (through September 1909). No-rivet-style rear axle on all 1909 models.

Colors—First 2,500 Cars: Touring: red or green. Runabout: gray. Town Car, Landaulet, and Coupe: green. Fenders, aprons, frame, and running gear painted body color. **From No. 2500:** Touring: red, green, some gray. Runabout: gray. Coupe, Town Car, and Landaulet: green. After June 1909, all cars were Brewster Green. Fenders, aprons, running boards, chassis, and running gear painted body color.

1910

Introduced in October 1909 and essentially the same as late-1909 cars.

Body Types and Prices

Touring	Runabout	Coupe	Town	Torpedo
$950	$900	$1,050	$1,200	—

The racy-looking Torpedo Runabout was a new Ford body style for 1910. It was the first Model T to have opening front doors on both sides. This 1911 model shows its semi-rectangular gas tank behind the body tub and curved rear fenders. The Torpedo's rakish style was achieved via a hood that was stretched 2 inches and a longer steering column set at a "faster" angle. *From the collections of The Henry Ford*

Noteworthy Features: Ford script with diamond shapes embossed into steel running boards. New method of fastening magnets to the flywheel; then larger flywheel to increase magneto power. Kingston L-2 as standard carburetor, but some Buffalo and Holley (No. 4150) carbs also used. Six-rivet-type rear axle.

Colors: All cars painted Brewster Green.

1911

Numerous engineering advances and two new body styles introduced in the 1911 Fords.

Body Types and Prices

Touring	Runabout	Coupe	Town	Torpedo
$780	$680	$1,050	$1,200	$725

Noteworthy Features: Sheet-steel body panels over hardwood frames became standard. Torpedo and open Runabout body styles introduced, the former with enclosed passenger compartment. Both types had different fenders, hoods, and running boards; the fuel tank moved to rear deck allowed seats to be moved rearward and mounted lower, for a "racier" feel and appearance. Removable engine oil pan (called a "connecting-rod pan") added, making lower-end servicing much easier. New cylinder-block casting featuring enclosed valve chambers. First Ford-made carburetor (the Model G) appeared, but Kingston remained standard. Magneto-powered electric conversion kits offered by the K-W Company for Ford gas headlamps (but Ford warned the T's magneto was not capable of powering the lights as well as the ignition system!).

Colors: All cars painted very dark blue, with black an option, although a small number of green Town Cars and red open Runabouts were built in April 1911, according to McCalley. Striping of fenders and running gear discontinued, though body striping continued through 1912.

1912
Two new, important body styles introduced.

One would expect any grocery store to be "sanitary," but Mr. Lavaque's new 1912 Delivery Car undoubtedly helped keep the goods from spoiling. The distinctive C-cab Delivery Car body was the precursor to the modern panel truck, but few were sold and the model became a one-year wonder. *From the collections of The Henry Ford*

Ford's five-car 1912 model range included a T for nearly every use. The Touring's drop in price from $850 in 1908 to $690 in 1912 is significant—although the assembly line was not yet in use, increases in productivity were already taking place. *From the collections of The Henry Ford*

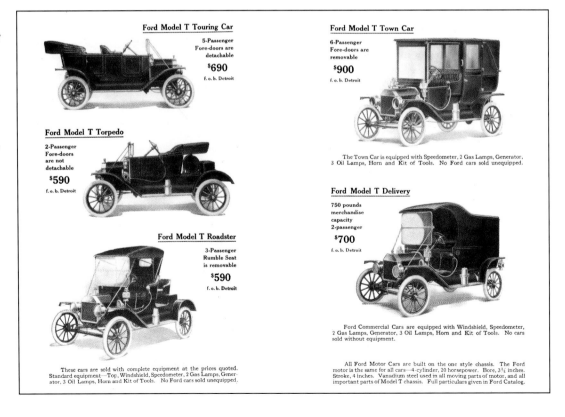

Ford Model T Touring Car
5-Passenger
Fore-doors are detachable
$690
f. o. b. Detroit

Ford Model T Torpedo
2-Passenger
Fore-doors are not detachable
$590
f. o. b. Detroit

Ford Model T Roadster
3-Passenger
Rumble Seat is removable
$590
f. o. b. Detroit

These cars are sold with complete equipment at the prices quoted. Standard equipment—Top, Windshield, Speedometer, 2 Gas Lamps, Generator, 3 Oil Lamps, Horn and Kit of Tools. No Ford cars sold unequipped.

Ford Model T Town Car
6-Passenger
Fore-doors are removable
$900
f. o. b. Detroit

The Town Car is equipped with Speedometer, 2 Gas Lamps, Generator, 3 Oil Lamps, Horn and Kit of Tools. No Ford cars sold unequipped.

Ford Model T Delivery
750 pounds merchandise capacity
2-passenger
$700
f. o. b. Detroit

Ford Commercial Cars are equipped with Windshield, Speedometer, 2 Gas Lamps, Generator, 3 Oil Lamps, Horn and Kit of Tools. No cars sold without equipment.

All Ford Motor Cars are built on the one style chassis. The Ford motor is the same for all cars—4-cylinder, 20 horsepower. Bore, 3¾ inches. Stroke, 4 inches. Vanadium steel used in all moving parts of motor, and all important parts of Model T chassis. Full particulars given in Ford Catalog.

The last Torpedoes were built for the 1912 model year, when this *Ford Times* advertisement appeared. They featured a new cylindrical gas tank. The lengthy, flexible brass air pipe from the rubber bulb to the horn was needed to clear the functional driver's door. *From the collections of The Henry Ford*

Body Types and Prices

Touring	Runabout	Town	Torpedo	Fore-Door
$690	$590	$900	—	—

Commercial
—

Noteworthy Features: New Fore-Door Touring Car body launched; its front (or fore) doors were factory items

and also made available for retrofits on earlier Touring Cars. Also, a revised Torpedo Runabout; a new Commercial (or Farm) Runabout with small rear cargo deck and detachable "mother-in-law" bucket seat; and the Delivery Car, the first Model T truck. This was the final year of the glorious, expensive, upright, brass windshield and the all-leather upholstery. Holley's H-1 was the most commonly used carburetor this year. Last year for the low-profile, "high-compression" (a measly 4.5:1!) cylinder head. Some heads in 1912 have "Made in USA" embossed in the casting.

Colors: Dark blue continued except on Delivery Cars, which were red with standard blue fenders at first, then offered with primered bodies and black fenders in early 1912.

1913
Cost reduction drove the move toward a more conservative, austere T. Final year for any parts supplied by the Dodge brothers.

For the 1913 model year, Ford replaced the Runabout's mother-in-law seat with the more practical and stylish "turtledeck" rear trunk compartment. Polished brass side-lamp bodies gave way to painted steel, one of many cost-reduction moves that would be seen at Highland Park that year. In this humorously posed 1914 publicity photo, driver and passenger appear quite pleased with the jaunty little flivver. Note the horizontal carbide-acetylene gas cylinder on the running board and the lack of any tread on the white rubber tires. *From the collections of The Henry Ford*

Body Types and Prices

Touring	Runabout	Town
$600	$525	$740

Noteworthy Features: First Touring with front doors and integral tonneau. First Runabout with rear "turtledeck" compartment—a classic styling cue that attracted hot rodders to the Model T many years later. Windshield frames now steel, and synthetic leatherette took over from real cowhide on the door inner panels.

Colors: Dark blue (with gray striping) continued for main bodies, with blue or black fenders, on 1913 model-year cars built in late 1912. Early in 1913, production black became Ford's one and only paint color available. Factory striping on bodies and fenders that had existed from the very first Model Ts was discontinued.

1914

Last year for the old-style Model T as Highland Park's rapidly rising production volumes bring prices down.

The huckster-type open body was a popular configuration on Model Ts for many years. The wooden bodies were available from a variety of specialist suppliers. This car, owned by grocer Hingham Supply Company, was photographed in 1914. The vehicle's easy access and general utility were loved by produce markets, street vendors, and tradesmen. *From the collections of The Henry Ford*

Body Types and Prices

Touring	Runabout	Coupe
$490	$440	$750

Noteworthy Features: Cast iron replaced aluminum on intake manifold. Last year for cherry-wood dashboard (firewall) and straight, flat fenders. Front fenders stamped with a stiffening rib across widest section. Each door had rounded bottom corners with revised latch handles. "Made in USA" added under Ford script on radiator shell and throughout the car on various parts.

1915

New "styling" introduced as engine compression ratio was reduced again. Larger magneto coils provided additional electrical output for new headlamps.

Above: The Coupelet, offered from 1915 to 1917, was Ford's first convertible coupe. The car's retractable top (leather in 1915, then leatherette) was felt-lined for a quality appearance and feel. The doors featured folding and removable pillars that served as window tracks when the glass was up and also folded flat across the window slot when the glass was retracted. Coupelets are among the most desirable Ts in the hobby today. *From the collections of The Henry Ford*

Opposite: The Model T was redesigned for 1915, and America's first low-priced sedan was added to the lineup. Its "center-door" body was designed with one hinged door amidships on each side. A more radiused cowl, magneto-powered headlamps, globe-like side lamps, and the switch to mostly faux-leather upholstery were other 1915 changes. The 1916 models were virtually carryover except steel hoods and lamp rims replaced the aluminum and brass items, respectively. The radiator shell was the only major brass component remaining—and it was finally replaced by a painted steel shell on 1917 cars. *From the collections of The Henry Ford*

Body Types and Prices

Touring	Runabout	Town	Sedan	Coupelet
$440	$390	$640	$740	$590

Noteworthy Features: Two new body styles introduced: the Sedan with two central side doors (known as the Center-door style) and the Coupelet, Ford's first convertible coupe. A steel cowl replaced the wood firewall, but the 1915 Centerdoor used aluminum exterior body panels to save weight. Rear fenders were curved for the first time on all body styles. Headlamps were 8 1/2-inch, 9-volt items in steel shells; hand Klaxon horn phased in through 1915 to replace the trusty old bulb horn. Louvers added to aluminum hood. Carburetors were Holley or Kingston. Leatherette took over for all upholstery on the open cars, except for a swatch of leather at major wear points on doors. Cloth upholstery ruled on closed cars.

1916

1915 styling continued, as leatherette took over inside the car.

Body Types and Prices

Touring	Runabout	Town	Sedan	Coupelet
$360	$345	$595	$640	$505

Noteworthy Features: Steel finally replaced aluminum in hood and radiator. Headlamps now painted black.

Above: The Town Car was perhaps the only Model T with any air of pretense. A luxury car it wasn't, lacking the power, heft, or cachet of true limousines. Indeed, its four doors were detachable. Ford produced only 11,303 units during the Town Car's 10-year run. It was perhaps the Lincoln Versailles of its day. *From the collections of The Henry Ford*

Below: With World War I underway, Victor Coubard operated a new Town Car as a taxi in Paris. Monsieur Coubard appears to be a decorated French soldier, and his use of the roomy, semi-closed T was fairly typical for this model. The tilting windshield was a handy feature in warm weather. *From the collections of The Henry Ford*

Gerhard "Jerk" Ritsema and the 1918 Runabout he bought for $75 in 1951 and has owned (and driven extensively) ever since. The 1918 Fords were essentially carryovers from 1917, the year they gained a revised front end with a taller steel radiator shell, larger hood, and more-contoured cowl. A new electric horn powered by the magneto was standard beginning in 1917. *Author photo*

1917

"New look" Model T gains an almost sleek appearance due to revised front-end sheet metal.

Body Types and Prices

Touring	Runabout	Town	Sedan	Coupelet
$360	$345	$595	$645	$505

Noteworthy Features: New exterior lines led by revised front end: high steel radiator shell now faired into larger hood, which better matched contour of the cowl. Fenders were curved and crowned. Engine compression was lowered again, this time to 3.98:1. Control pedals lost their markings, and were now smooth-surfaced. Tapered roller bearings replaced balls in front wheel hubs and spindles. Electric horn powered by the magneto became standard.

1918

No major changes, except many cars fitted with square-ended leaf springs in addition to the regular tapered-end springs. Coupelet and Town Cars offered for the last time.

Body Types and Prices

Touring	Runabout	Sedan	Coupelet	Town Car
$525	$500	$775	$650	$645

One of the Model T's most recognizable styling cues was the turtledeck rear trunk, shown here on a 1918 Runabout. It was a separate unit on Runabouts but became integral with the body on Coupes beginning in 1923. *Author photo*

For the 1918 model year, the Coupelet evolved into a "hardtop coupe" with flat roof and tall cabin. The new model was fitted with folding and removable window pillars similar to those used in the previous Coupelets. Lowering the windows with a leather strap and removing the pillars eliminated the car's quarter windows and dramatically widened the window openings—nice for driving on a warm day. The photos show the 1918 Coupelet owned by western Michigan Model T expert and collector Gerhard "Jerk" Ritsema, along with details of an open door with pillars upright and removed. Ritsema knows of only five other surviving examples of this rare model. His car earned a place in Ford Motor Company's 2003 Centennial Circle in Dearborn. Models from 1919 did not include the removable window pillars. *Author photos*

1919

Electric starter (closed cars only) and demountable rims offered as optional equipment.

Body Types and Prices

Touring	Runabout	Sedan	Coupe
$525	$500	$775	$650

Noteworthy Features: To fit the starter system, the engine flywheel was modified to accept a ring gear; the cylinder block and timing-gear cover were altered to support and drive the six-volt generator from the camshaft gear; and the transmission cover was revamped to accept the starter motor. Timing gears were changed from straight-cut to helical-type to reduce lash and gear noise. Electric-start Fords were also fitted with an electric tail lamp (this became a popular accessory for the pre-electric-start magneto cars). Demountable "clincher" rims for 30x3 1/2-inch tires were optional for the closed cars only; standard front tires remained 30x4 inches.

1920

Styling remained unchanged from the 1917 body forms, except Sedans were fitted with a dashboard that included an ammeter and a combination ignition switch/light mounted on an escutcheon plate. Stewart speedometers optional.

Body Types and Prices

	Touring	Runabout	Sedan	Coupe
(March)	$575	$550	$975	$850
(September)	$440	$395	$795	$745

Noteworthy Features: To prepare for the change to lowered bodies, early in 1920 the original cylindrical gas tank was changed to a new oval cross-section type for all bodies except Sedans, which still used the square tank as fitted to many early Coupes. Steering-wheel diameter increased to 16 inches, with a stamped-steel spider replacing the previous cast item. Demountable rims now optional ($21) on all Fords.

1921

A year of very minor mechanical changes.

Body Types and Prices

	Touring	Runabout	Sedan	Coupe
(June)	$415	$370	$760	$695
(September)	$355	$325	$660	$595

Noteworthy Features: Front engine support and front spring clamp now forged into a single unit. Kingston model L-4 carburetor adopted on many (but not all) engines from 1921 to 1922.

1922

No changes in body style from previous year.

Body Types and Prices

Touring	Runabout	Sedan	Coupe
$348	$319	$645	$580

Noteworthy Features: Sedan bodies with two centrally located doors and oval window appeared for the last time.

1923

New styling for the 1923 model year was launched in August 1922.

Body Types and Styles

Touring	Runabout	Sedan (two-door)	Sedan (four-door)	Coupe
$393	$364	$595	$725	$530

Noteworthy Features: Lowered bodies, in the works since 1919, heralded the first major restyle since 1917. All body types had a taller radiator that included an apron at the bottom of the radiator shell. Ford offered two Sedan body types for the first time: a two-door and four-door, the latter with rear-hinged ("suicide-type") rear doors. Four-door Sedans also received aluminum body panels (still over a hardwood frame) to replace the heavier steel. Fords gained weight as they added more features. The rear compartments of the Coupes were integrated with the body and a large rectangular rear window, plus rotary window regulators, cowl-ventilator door, and square gas tank. Runabouts still had their turtledeck compartments separate from the body to enable the car to be sold as a "chassis" model for commercial use. Open cars had the windshield set at a "faster" (more rakish)

Ford gave the T another mild restyling in 1923, and those visual upgrades carried over to 1925, the year this Tudor owned by Ron Flockstra was built. Most of the changes made between 1918 and 1925 are noticeable only when closely comparing cars side by side and were not really enough to create a truly fresh appearance. Even the revamped 1926–1927 models didn't quite succeed at that. *Author photo*

angle and a new "one-man" top (advertised as allowing one person to erect it).

1924

No major changes from 1923, as the mighty Ford production system hit overdrive, squeezing yet more cost out of the vehicle and enabling the lowest retail prices yet.

Body Types and Prices

Touring	Runabout	Sedan (two-door)	Sedan (four-door)	Coupe
$295	$265	$590	$685	$525

Noteworthy Features: Final year for open cars available with the 30x3-inch clincher front tires.

1925

Minor changes from the 1923 styles, including first use of "balloon" tires and windshield wipers (hand-operated). New nameplates adopted for the two-door (Tudor) and four-door (Fordor) sedans.

Body Types and Prices

Touring	Runabout	Tudor	Fordor	Coupe
$290	$260	$580	$660	$520

Ford offered its first factory-built pickup truck in 1925. It was basically a Runabout with a pickup bed bolted onto the turtledeck platform behind the body tub. Customers had two options: buy the Runabout and a separate pickup bed ($25) from your Ford dealer and make the conversion yourself, or buy a pickup complete and ready to haul for $281 ($21 more than the standard Runabout). Ford sold nearly 34,000 factory-built pickups in 1925, and a legend was born. *From the collections of The Henry Ford*

Noteworthy Features: The 4.4x21-inch balloon tires were a $25 option. Last year for small rear brake drums and cast-iron brake shoes. Also last year in which open cars were available with hand-crank starter, magneto-powered headlamps, and rear oil tail lamp introduced in 1915 (some Luddite customers were undoubtedly disappointed). Steel continued to replace hardwood in body framing.

1926

Beginning with the 12,225,528th Model T produced in November 1925, Ford ushered in the most profound styling change in the Tin Lizzie's history—and Ford brought back color choices! By July 1926, T production had reached the 14 million mark.

Body Types and Prices

Touring	Runabout	Tudor	Fordor	Coupe
$380	$360	$495	$545	$485

Noteworthy Features: Chassis height lowered 1 1/2 inches by lowering the rear spring crown the same distance and the front spring crown by 1 inch. Of course there was an exception: the Tudor body was lowered an additional 2 1/2 inches (total 4 inches). The new, more rounded radiator shell boasted nickel plating, as did the headlamp shells. (Beginning January 1926, the headlamps were mounted on a crossbar between the front fenders.) The radiator shell was 5/8 inch higher and mated with a longer hood (with more louvers) that sloped nicely into the cowl. Bodies were lengthened 3 1/2 inches and combined with more crown on the now-beadless fenders. The old flivver looked almost modern. Drivers finally could enter the car through a new hinged door on the left side. Runabout rear compartments were integrated with their bodies, and Coupe and Tudor models received a new one-piece windshield. To complement the slicker bodywork, Ford brought back a choice of paint colors (blue, brown, and gray) after a decade of somber black-only Ford cars!

In an effort to improve throttle response, lightweight cast-iron pistons were fitted. The fuel tank was relocated to the cowl on all models except the Fordor (still with its square tank under the front seat). To compensate for the increased turning resistance of the fatter balloon tires, the 1926 T was given a larger-diameter (17 inches) steering wheel. In the name of safety, the car's brake drums (still rear-wheel-only)

The 1926–1927 Model Ts were known as "the Improved Fords," and indeed they were the company's late attempt at playing catch-up with Chevrolet and others in terms of styling and features. Ford brought back paint-color choices and brightwork (nickel-plated radiator shells), made balloon tires standard, phased in standard steel wire wheels, and offered a long list of subtle changes and optional equipment, including shock absorbers, stop lights, and automatic windshield wipers. But the improved Lizzies, such as this (restored) pickup with its longer-radius front fenders, continued with the 20-horsepower engine, transmission brake, and two-speed planetary transmission. The changing market and competitors' advancements made these models the last Ts. *Artemis Images*

were significantly increased in diameter from 8 to 11 inches and in width from 1 5/32 to 1 1/2 inches.

1927

In the final year of Model T production, the cars remained largely unchanged from 1926, except for the addition of a wire-wheel option. The color palette was also expanded to include green and maroon. In June 1927, the Model T production line was shut down to begin the long retool for the Model A, after 15,007,033 units had been built.

Body Types and Prices

Touring	Runabout	Tudor	Fordor	Coupe
$380	$360	$495	$545	$485

In the eyes of many, the Model T was a blank canvas—simply a workhorse platform upon which a traveler's dreams could be built. This early attempt at a motor home was built shortly after World War I by the creative, although nameless, Texans shown here. They traveled many miles in their little home on wheels before and after this photo was snapped in 1921. *From the collections of The Henry Ford*

Chapter 4

LIFE WITH LIZZIE

Owning and driving the Model T

Learning to drive a Model T was an unforgettable and usually thrilling experience for millions of people during the first three decades of the twentieth century. Often the Ford was their initiation into the automobile age. In making the transition from four-legged horsepower to a T, there were a few old habits to unlearn: yanking on leather reins, cracking a buggy whip, and mastering those loud clicking commands to get reluctant hoofs moving. These were soon replaced with "Fill 'er up and check the oil!"

Talking to the car as if it were alive while starting, driving, and performing maintenance also became familiar carryovers for former horse-and-buggy owners. Many early T owners missed their beloved beasts of burden as traveling companions, and they quickly bestowed names on their cars that were in many ways no less colorful or endearing than the animals'.

Henry Ford recognized that making the car easy to operate was critical to its mass appeal. This was one reason why he championed the two-speed planetary transmission with its three-pedal control. And Ford wasn't alone in his thinking. A feature on transmission trends in *The Automobile* published prior to the T's 1908 debut noted that pedal-operated planetary gearboxes were by far the most popular type in cars costing less than $1,500. (The planetary transmission is the granddaddy of today's automatic. Although it doesn't have a torque converter, it uses foot-pedal pressure, rather than hydraulic pressure, to operate the bands controlling low, high, and reverse gears.)

With 19 years of automotive know-how between them, the 1906 Model N and 1925 Tudor sedan differed in their steering wheel locations and equipment levels. But the two Fords still shared much in terms of basic design, function, and operation—the result of Henry Ford's mandates to keep the Model T simple, light, and affordable. *From the collections of The Henry Ford*

Ford's vision paid off. Learning to drive a Model T "was sublimely and absurdly simple" compared with most of its contemporaries, noted Philip Stern in his 1955 book, *Tin Lizzie*. Even today, for a relatively few mechanically oriented, open-minded folks, the T can be mastered without much fuss.

For drivers in 2008, most of whom were weaned on slick automatic transmissions, power steering and brakes, and effortless starting, however, getting behind the wheel of a T and easing it out into traffic might be a counterintuitive,

daunting experience. (Driving any vehicle of the T's era in modern traffic generally demands more attention to controls and operation than today's cars and trucks.)

Pull yourself up onto the Model T driver's perch and you'll be sitting at approximately the same height as in a modern 4x4 pickup truck. Slipping across the thickly padded seat, you will immediately reach for a track adjuster to give more legroom. But the seat position and backrest are fixed, which has made getting comfortable in a Model T a perennial challenge for many taller drivers.

TAKING A T TO THE DMV

Few rites of passage are as eagerly anticipated by teenagers as obtaining a driver's license. Like most 16-year-olds, Robert Panish, a resident of California's San Fernando Valley, had his choice of which family vehicle he wanted to use to take his driving test in late 2000. Unlike most, he chose the family's 1923 Model T Touring.

A quick telephone call to a nearby Department of Motor Vehicles office confirmed there would be no objection. From the crank start to the ride in the Model T, the offbeat experience was a pleasure for licensing examiner Mark Morefield.

"Robert achieved just about the best score I've ever given anyone," Morefield reported later. And to properly "frost the cake," after young Panish's achievement, his parents presented him with his very own Model T: a 1914 Speedster with personalized plates, 14T 4 RMP.

When the Tin Lizzie turned 100 years old, Robert Panish, master's degree in hand, commenced work on his astro-aero engineering doctorate at MIT. Although he plans to work on developing future spacecraft, Model Ts will always have a special place in his life. Henry Ford would understand and be proud.

Sixteen-year-old Robert Panish takes his California driver's test in 2000, driving his family's 1923 Touring. DMV examiner Mark Morefield is with him. The car is equipped with aftermarket front coil springs and appropriate license plate. *Helen V. Hutchings*

But not for Steven Rossi. The 6-foot-4-inch antique-vehicle hobbyist is plenty comfy while romping his 1924 Coupe over hill and dale of rural Connecticut on a close-to-daily basis.

"One reason I bought a Model T rather than the larger, more modern Model A is I can't fit in an A!" he said. "Its gearshift lever is literally underneath my right kneecap. I find the T's cockpit is much more open and roomy than a Model A's."

When Ford finally offered an electric starter in 1919, the $70 option was worth nearly three weeks' pay for a Highland Park factory worker. But the "electric arm" made living with a T much easier, and it helped expand Ford sales, particularly with women. Some customers did not trust the newfangled starter, however. They preferred the familiar, proven hand crank located near the base of the car's radiator.

Cranking a Model T "was a special trick, and until you learned it (usually from another Ford owner, but sometimes by a period of appalling experimentation) you might as well have been winding up an awning," noted authors E. B. White and Richard L. Strout in "Farewell, My Lovely," their famous collaborative tribute to the Model T published in *The New Yorker* in 1936. White knew the T intimately,

Henry Ford loved to prove the Model T's mettle in front of the camera. In this 1916 scene, he and his veteran test driver and factory hotshoe, Frank Kulick, show the advantages of high ground clearance as they coax a mud-splattered Touring along the "wet side" of a northern Michigan lake. The water level is nearly parallel to the front frame rail, which is at carburetor-intake height. *From the collections of The Henry Ford*

having traveled across the United States in one as a college graduate in 1922.

John Steinbeck, who witnessed the T's role in the great westward migration of the 1930s during his reporting for *The Grapes of Wrath*, claimed that the Model T sensed exactly the number of crank turns he would tolerate before he wanted to smash the car's radiator in frustration.

The starting process is simple (see page 101), but as when kick-starting some motorcycles, there are precautions to guard against getting hurt. When cranking a T, you should not wrap your thumb around the crank handle because a backfire can cause the handle to abruptly kick back in the opposite direction, potentially breaking your thumb or spraining your wrist or elbow, as more than a few T owners can attest.

"You've got to approach hand-cranking with a certain degree of caution and respect," said antique Ford enthusiast John Forster, whose red 1909 Touring graces this book's cover.

In the depths of winter, hand-cranking a T was no mean feat. With thickened oil in the sump, there were various recommended solutions for starting, including cranking the engine with one rear wheel jacked up off the ground, or building a small fire underneath the pan to warm up the oil.

Electrically heated intake manifolds were available, as were manifold covers incorporating cups into which a small quantity of gasoline or alcohol would be poured. When a flame was applied under the cups, the manifold warmed up sufficiently so the engine cranked easily—in theory. But as legendary Model T technical maven Murray Fahnestock cautioned in 1923, "care should be taken not to flood the carburetor or attempt to start the engine until the flame is completely burned out. Otherwise there is more or less risk in setting the engine on fire."

Also, if the emergency brake isn't fully deployed during starting, the car has an odd habit of creeping forward.

"There was never a moment when the [transmission] bands were not faintly egging the machine on," noted White and Strout. Early owners would liken this to being nuzzled by a horse, and if the car was on level ground, it could be prevented from moving simply by leaning against the radiator.

Slower Traffic Keep Right

When it was introduced in late 1908, the Model T was perhaps the sprightliest car of its class in the world, thanks to its

CRANK 'ER UP!
A proven crank-starting drill

In truth, the T was a willing and reliable starter. As numerous T owners have demonstrated to the author, a proven crank-starting drill is as follows:

Pull the handbrake lever back until snug. This also puts the gearbox into neutral.

Open the throttle lever on the right side of the steering column to the fifth or sixth notch.

Slide the ignition-advance lever on the left side of the steering column fully "up" (retarded).

Move to the front of the car and pull the loop on the end of the carburetor choke wire that protrudes through the front of the car's radiator.

Spin the crank handle a couple of times to turn the engine over so one piston is near top dead center. (Many owners suggest this is a good time to say a few encouraging words to the car, particularly in cold or rainy weather.)

Walk to the dashboard and switch the ignition on.

Walk back to the front of the car and give the crank a serious spin.

As the engine pops into life, release the choke, sprint to the driver's side of the cockpit (or reach in from the passenger's side), move the ignition lever down a couple of notches, and adjust the throttle lever to achieve a smooth idle.

If the engine does not start, talk to the car in a different manner. In cold or rainy weather, prayer sometimes works.

Mike Ritsema expertly spins the crank on his homebuilt speedster. *Author photo*

torquey engine and downright feathery curb weight. Owners found that the original powertrain handled almost any road or load thrown its way, including serving in the TT truck chassis (see Chapter 5). Even the car's marginal transmission-band brake was remarkably up to the job of stopping the car in the light road traffic of the time (the first traffic lights didn't appear in major cities until 1914).

But by the 1930s, the Ford powertrain was outclassed by improved roads, heavier traffic, and a generally faster pace. *continued on page 104*

For many early automobile owners, the car dealer was their lifeline to keeping the vehicle on the road. Direct correspondence with the factory was often required to obtain parts, and waiting for them (often for weeks) was common. The advent of the easy-to-maintain Model T transformed that experience with widespread availability of low-cost parts from an expansive network of Ford dealers, such as this one in Newark, Ohio, with a new Torpedo Runabout, circa 1912. *From the collections of The Henry Ford*

The Model T on a Teeter

At a recent fair in Seattle, Manager Rice, in his FORD car, was the only one who was able to balance on the teeter. This was owing to the very simple control of the FORD car

Through its regional distributors and local dealers, Ford regularly staged zany demonstrations to prove the T's ease of operation. This one was held at the 1910 Seattle State Fair and must have required some deft pedalwork to gingerly balance the car on the "sweet spot" of the rocking teeter. *From the collections of The Henry Ford*

continued from page 101
Still, the Model T soldiered on for many thousands of loyal owners whose main concern was basic transportation—and for those who couldn't afford a better car.

Steve Rossi put the T's performance into perspective in 2008: "If you try to push the Model T into today's driving environment on billiard-smooth surfaces, it falls way short. That's why the car is so enjoyable on dirt or gravel country roads, slowing down and maneuvering around potholes and using its 30-inch wheels and ample ground clearance, which is how it functioned in its day. This is a 20-horsepower car capable of 35 miles per hour; you just have to drive around the power that it has."

When you put the T back into its original environment, it works exceptionally well, Rossi asserted. "Letting the car operate at its own pace, it does everything it was designed to

A Model T was the first gasoline-powered machine that many farmers purchased in the decade prior to World War I. Ford Runabouts like this well-used 1912 model served as rural America's link to church, town, and broader social and business lives. The T also was very popular with rural doctors and veterinarians, who used the cars to get to their patients. Note the car's optional side curtains. *From the collections of The Henry Ford*

do," he said. "It's got a nice, fat torque curve, and when it's in the middle of that curve the car will really surprise you as it chugs up hills. From that viewpoint you can clearly see how Ford sold 15 million of them."

Of course, things can get busy for the driver who is faced with three foot pedals to engage the forward gear ratios plus reverse and brake; separate throttle and spark levers under the steering wheel; and a floor-mounted lever controlling neutral (while in the upright position), second gear (when in the forward position while the left pedal is not depressed), and the parking brake (when pulled all the way back).

Combine this setup with manual steering that's *heavy* at slow speeds, and driving a Model T demands supreme concentration in modern traffic. This is not a car that forgives its driver for using a mobile phone and gobbling a sandwich while steering with one knee!

In one of the early manuals on Model T care and operation, the driver was instructed to hold the left pedal in a midway position, open the hand throttle a certain number of notches on the quadrant, depress the pedal, run 20 feet (in low gear), then let the pedal spring back into high gear. This was all fine for a level road, but to start on an upgrade required a wider

In addition to providing motive power, the T was widely used as a stationary power source. In this 1910 scene, a farmer has enlisted his Touring to run a grain mill in the barn. The Ford was far easier to manage than a mule for such operations, and nearly as cheap to maintain. *From the collections of The Henry Ford*

opening of the throttle and a longer run, whereas on a downgrade, less throttle and a shorter run would suffice.

Needless to say, people who drove "by the book" found themselves stalling on an upgrade and making excessive noise on the downgrade until they were reeducated by a more experienced T owner.

"It's totally foreign to you in the beginning, when you step out of a modern car," said 1924 Touring owner David

Jones. "But after you get used to it you don't have to think about it. It's easy to drive once you get the hang of it. The best advice is to plan ahead, especially when braking!"

Anticipating fuel stops was another critical aspect of T ownership. With its 9-gallon gas tank located underneath the front seat, occupants had to disembark when fill-up time arrived. "Refueling was more of a social function then, because the driver had to unbend, whether he wanted to or

As Model T sales exploded, a variety of aftermarket kits expanded its many uses. Staude's Mak-a-Tractor converted Ford's Runabout into a gutsy little tractor with the addition of large-diameter steel drive wheels and a rear power takeoff. In this 1919 photo, a farmer steers the T while his young son operates a McCormick-Deering grain reaper. *From the collections of The Henry Ford*

Another T-based Staude Mak-a-Tractor earns its keep, this time pulling a multi-gang plow near St. Paul, Minnesota. Such extreme use could present durability problems due to the Ford's lack of standard air filtration and water pump. *From the collections of The Henry Ford*

not," observed White and Strout. (In cold weather, a gas stop meant digging oneself out from underneath woolen blankets brought along for warmth.)

"You're thinking this little lightweight car is getting 40 miles per gallon when, really, it's getting about 15 miles per gallon," explained Rossi. "Model Ts don't get good fuel economy in relative terms compared with today's small cars. So you end up using more gas than you realize, and when you drive the car regularly you have to be careful not to run out of fuel."

Model T owners have always carried a wooden measuring stick to gauge the depth of gas in the tank, although that task is often handled by simply unscrewing the cap and peering into the vaporous darkness. Fitting an aftermarket speedometer with a resettable odometer is another method of monitoring driving range.

Running out of gas was a real issue during the T's heyday. The problem was often caused by the car's lack of a fuel pump; on steep grades the T's engine could encounter fuel starvation. A common solution was to drive backward up hills.

While this *Ford Times* image from September 1913 appears to have been mildly retouched, it no doubt accurately portrays yet another application of Model T power. This time it's a Melbourne, Australia, equine groomer using 22 Ford horses and belt drive to shear a rather bored-looking stallion. *From the collections of The Henry Ford*

The author's grandmother, Elizabeth Hughes Brooke, was one of the first women on Philadelphia's Main Line to own a car, having inherited her nearly new Model T Runabout when her father passed away prior to World War I. She loved to recall piloting "my Lizzie" (her nickname for the car) up hilly County Line Road in reverse gear in order to get home on low fuel.

Driving after dark also brought its own peculiarities in a Model T. In 1915, Ford replaced the car's original carbide headlamps with magneto-powered electric lamps. The illumination of these units rose and fell according to engine speed—the higher the rpm, the brighter the light. Owners sometimes plodded along in low gear at night because it provided the brightest, albeit slowest, path home.

Compared with most cars of the 1920s, the T offered its driver little, if any, visual information on its internal operating status, other than what he or she could hear, feel, or smell. Though the speedometer was an option beginning in 1909, not all cars were so equipped, and there were no temperature, fuel, or oil-pressure gauges. Later cars added an ammeter, the needle of which tended to gyrate wildly with engine speed. All of the missing equipment was eventually served by the aftermarket.

"The Ford driver flew blind," noted White and Strout, who added that "owners had their own theories about everything; they discussed mutual problems in that wise, infinitely resourceful way old women discuss rheumatism. Exact knowledge was pretty scarce, and often proved less effective than superstition."

The accessories produced specifically for the Model T during the car's 19-year production run could fill a book of their own. Improving the car's buckboard ride quality with supplemental coil springs and various types of suspension dampeners was the focus of many manufacturers, including Bosch. *Author collection*

Conversely, the T was the most repairable car of its day. If the resourceful owner supplemented the standard Ford tool kit with a pipe wrench, a coil of baling wire, a tire-patch kit, a spare inner tube and tire irons, perhaps some bobby pins, and a pocketknife, he or she could tackle practically any mechanical problem that arose on the road.

California or Bust

The sheer number of Model Ts produced ensured that the car would remain a fixture on American roads long after production ended, albeit in declining numbers. Through the latter half of the Roaring Twenties it became common to

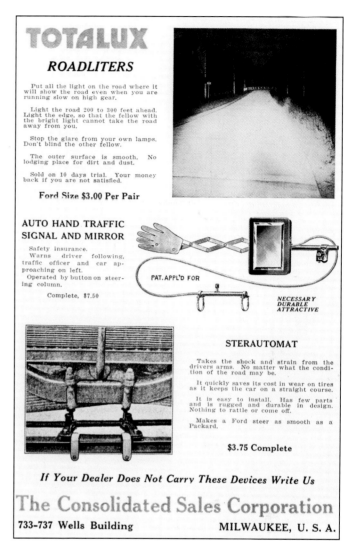

"Makes a Ford steer as smooth as a Packard!" was typical of the hype that helped sell countless widgets, doo-dads, Auto Hand Traffic Signals, and even many legitimately useful Model T accessories. Period automotive publications were filled with pages like this one from February 1917. *From the collections of The Henry Ford*

hear people say they were tired of being one of the masses; they yearned to lift themselves out of the "Ford class."

Such remarks indicated that the car-buying public was moving beyond elemental, low-cost vehicles. Certainly by the time the Great Depression was hammering America in the 1930s, the T had become a used car. Examples in running condition were widely available for as little as $10.

Styling kits gave Model T owners the chance to personalize their cars. Many considered items such as the popular V-radiator shells (shown here on a restored Runabout at a Model T club rally) to be the modernizations that Ford itself seemed reluctant or unwilling to do. *Artemis Images*

In the eyes of many, the T was the automotive symbol of the down-and-out. Scores of poor migrants from the dust bowl of Oklahoma, Texas, and the Deep South drove dilapidated Fords—crushingly overloaded with family, provisions, and furniture—along Route 66 toward what they hoped would be the "land of milk and honey" in California's farm belt.

Amid the westbound tide, the "Okies" and their Ts were undeservedly treated as pariahs in some areas. To discourage the lowly Ford owners, nefarious campground owners reportedly charged many times the standard night's rate to keep out the flood of battered black flivvers.

Accessories Galore

Not only did the Model T make Henry Ford an immensely wealthy man, it also spawned a booming aftermarket estimated to have been worth more than $60 million at its peak during the mid-1920s.

Hundreds of manufacturers catered to dolling up and improving the T. They served up many features—including speed, oil, and temperature gauges; shock absorbers; better brakes; air filters; electric starters; and battery-and-coil ignitions—that the automaker should have included through the years. In the many mail-order catalogs of the day, indulgent owners could find everything from anti-rattle door latches to

Does a Model T need a water pump and greater cooling capacity or not? That question has been a hot topic ever since the T's inception. Certainly, water pump kits such as this one marketed by Staude were extremely popular during the T's heyday. Other makers included Neupert, Sta-Kool, Red Arrow, Niagara, and Reliable. *From the collections of The Henry Ford*

The T's basic proportions and ample ground clearance made it relatively simple to fit it with flanged railroad wheels, turning the flivver into a track-inspection car. The Touring in this mildly retouched 1916 photograph was used by the Indiana Harbor Belt Railroad. *From the collections of The Henry Ford*

kits for converting a Tourer into a camper. Sears, Roebuck and Company, in particular, carried page after page of Ford items.

To illustrate the breadth of aftermarket accessories in the 1920s, for about $100 the speed-thirsty T owner could buy a Craig-Hunt cylinder head with four overhead valves per cylinder—serious high-quality racing hardware (see Chapter 6). For $16, there was the Neville "More-Room" lockable steering wheel. Nicknamed the "fat-man wheel," these walnut-rimmed wheels were nicely engineered to swing out of the way for easier ingress and egress. Fat-man wheels were especially popular on Coupes and closed Sedans.

At the other extreme were trainloads of gizmos and gadgets. Some were marginally useful, but many were cheesy junk hawked by fly-by-night vendors. Typical of the many

continued on page 116

Moving railcars was another vocation that the Fords tackled successfully, as long as the track grades were moderate and the payloads light. In this 1920s photograph, it appears that a railway T loaded with lawmen or government officials is about to lead a convoy of similarly configured Fords out of a southwestern U.S. railyard. *From the collections of The Henry Ford*

The Model T provided mobility and opened new horizons for millions of people who had never left the farm. Road trips begat "car camping," and this 1915 scene is hardly different from hitting the road with car and tent today. *From the collections of The Henry Ford*

The Touring was the most versatile T when it came to passenger accommodations. As this 1914 article in *The Fordowner* showed, a bit of effort and a few simple materials converted the Ford into a motel on wheels. *From the collections of The Henry Ford*

A variation on the mobile home theme was Reverend Branford Clarke's chapel-on-wheels. Based in New York during the 1920s, Reverend Clarke took the Gospel on the road in his T-based sanctuary, which contained a small organ. He designed the steeple to fold down, enabling him to garage the rig. *From the collections of The Henry Ford*

Automobile expeditions to exotic regions were big news during the Model T's heyday, and Fords were in the thick of the activity. Controversial globetrotter and suspected con man Valerian Johannes Tieczynski, who called himself Captain Walter Wanderwell, led motor car tours of Europe, the Middle East, and Asia, one of them in this specially modified T. He was accompanied by his 23-year-old lover, Galcia Hall (who went by the name Aloha Wanderwell and told the press she was Wanderwell's sister). He was murdered years later while preparing for another journey. *From the collections of The Henry Ford*

continued from page 111

questionable improvements was the Speedler, which sold for $5. A perforated tube with three small ports at the end, it was screwed into the Model T's intake manifold. The ports were opened and closed via a cable leading to a small lever on the steering column. As the Ford gained speed, opening the ports allowed air to enter the manifold, boosting airflow without further opening the throttle.

In effect, the Speedler altered the mixture in a way not possible with the simple float carburetor. On descending a hill on closed throttle, the driver opened the Speedler, increasing engine braking and helping to cool the engine, or so the manufacturer touted. The claimed net effect was up to 10 miles per gallon greater fuel economy at cruising speed—a considerable gain if the Speedler ads were true.

Brake upgrades were one of the most popular and effective modifications sold for Ford cars. "Since most automobiles have been born in level Detroit, that is the reason so many cars have deficient brakes," reasoned T tech guru Murray Fahnestock in 1925. Transmission brake bands with more durable lining material were sold to replace the stock cotton linings. But the biggest improvement for slowing the car came in various brake kits that converted the car's feeble 7-inch (11-inch in 1926–1927) rear parking brakes into service brakes operated by the car's foot pedal.

There were external-contracting types made by a variety of aftermarket vendors including Rocky Mountain, Jumbo, Rishmuller, APCO, Royal, Brooklyn, A-C, Cleveland, Mohawk, Perfection, and Reese. Internal-expanding drum brakes, their basic operation similar to today's drums (except for their lack of hydraulic actuation), were offered by Rusco, Stephens, Bailey, and Warford (for TT trucks), among others.

Of all the aftermarket binders, the Rocky Mountain units were perhaps the best known. Fitted on oversized 12 1/4-inch drums, they provided more than 103 square inches of braking surface, compared with the paltry 23 square inches provided by the stock 7-inch Ford brakes. The California-based Rocky

Owners from all over the world who racked up extraordinarily high mileages in their Model Ts made regular pilgrimages to Highland Park. This well-worn Touring is shown in front of the great factory wearing a variety of U.S. state and college pennants picked up along the way. *From the collections of The Henry Ford*

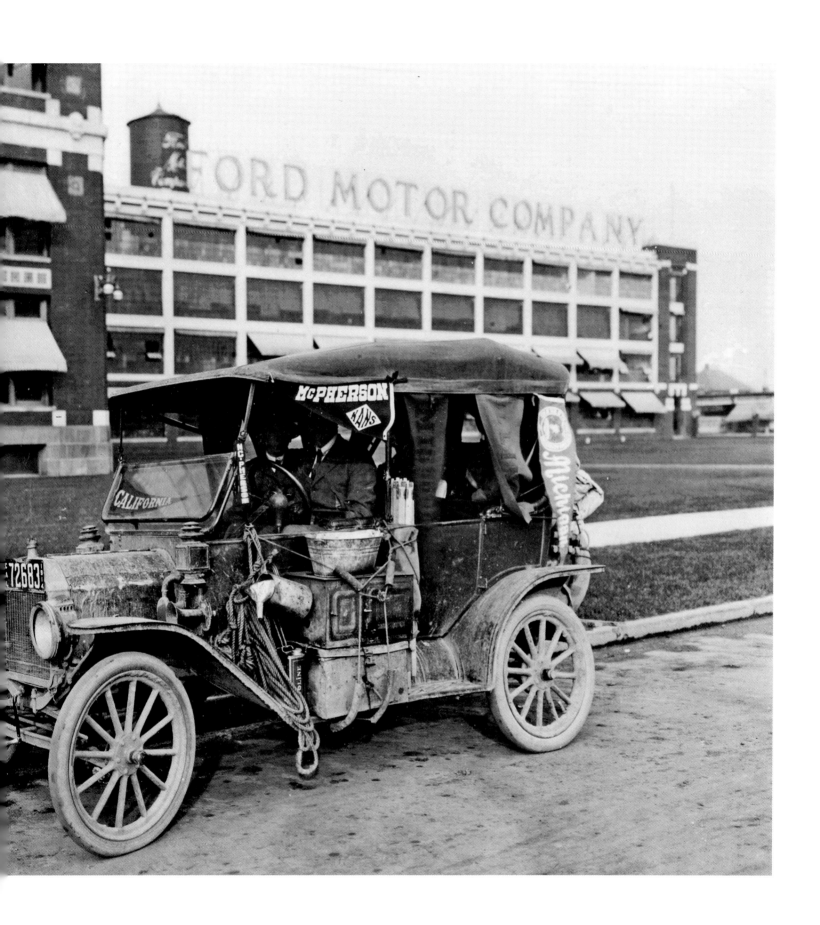

Even in the 1940s, T owners trekked to Detroit, some of them hoping to proudly show their tough old flivvers to Henry Ford himself. These two Argentineans lucked out on the return leg of their 1941 "Buenos Aires to New York" tour, when the aging company founder happily met them and posed with their car. *From the collections of The Henry Ford*

Mountain company also made special spring perches for installing its big brakes on Ts upgraded with aftermarket rear shock absorbers. Reproduction Rocky Mountain brakes are available today for Model Ts (see Chapter 7).

A Model T owner would have wanted Rocky Mountain brakes if he or she wished for improved performance. There were many ways to do this, including fitting a sliding-gear-type auxiliary transmission (made by Himico, Woodward, Brooklyn, Warford, Rocky Mountain, and others) or two-speed rear axle. These setups were popular on T trucks (see Chapter 5), but many cars (particularly the heavier Tourers, Tudors, and Fordors) also benefited from the addition of more gear ratios. A T so equipped might be capable of 50 miles per hour (with a tailwind), with improved pulling and hillclimbing power.

Ruckstell two-speed rear axles and Rocky Mountain brakes were the peanut butter and jelly of Model T performance enhancements, and the two are often paired on restored Ts

Model Ts were cut, shaped, and otherwise morphed into every configuration imaginable. Why spend for a proper bus when two used Fords, some pieces of steel, and a welding torch will get you the same thing? This is the fully loaded MacKay's *Daytona-to-Deland Express*, about to depart the Halifax River Yacht Club near Daytona Beach in 1921. *From the collections of The Henry Ford*

Snow-tractor conversions were another Frankensteinian idea, this one relying on the basic Model T chassis and drivetrain to power a pair of tracked bogies. This prototype seen under test in 1921 differs from the commercial rigs shown in Chapter 7 in that it does not use skids in front. *From the collections of The Henry Ford*

Henry Ford presented this 1916 Touring car to his friend and mentor Thomas Edison, seen here, and is said to have assigned a team of Ford mechanics to regularly maintain and upgrade it over the years. *From the collections of The Henry Ford*

today. Designed during the World War I period, the Ruckstell was a planetary gearset that fit inside a special housing attached to one side of the stock Ford differential. When combined with the T's two-speed gearbox, the Ruckstell gave four nicely spaced forward ratios. Installation could be done with a few hand tools in a few hours.

Another favorite period accessory was a water pump, along with a larger and more efficient cooling fan. Dozens of pump kits were offered in the 1920s, although these are controversial with T enthusiasts today. As noted previously, Ford's original engine design incorporated a gear-driven water pump, which was fitted to approximately the first

2,500 cars built through early 1909. At that point, Henry Ford and his designers felt the pump unnecessary and modified the engine design to incorporate the famous pumpless "thermo-siphon" cooling system.

"The T's cooling system works best just before it gets hot enough to boil the water," commented owner David Jones, who also has driven various Ts in the bustling Greenfield Village fleet through some of Michigan's hottest summers. "If the engine starts to 'tea kettle,' the solution is simply to run it faster!"

Some T experts believe accessory water pumps can cause problems because they tend to move the liquid faster than the radiator can cool it. Cavitation (excess air bubbles) is another woe associated with accessory pumps.

"The car doesn't need a water pump, which is why Ford removed his!" asserts Gerhard "Jerk" Ritsema. In his nearly 60 years of Model T ownership, including a 1955 whirlwind journey from western Michigan to California in his 1914 Touring, Ritsema has found the thermo-siphon system lives up to Ford's high standards in all types of driving.

Fitted with a variety of commercial bodies, the stout little T trucks' ability to perform far beyond their payload ratings made them popular choices in the agricultural and construction trades. This one was photographed hauling 8,000 pounds of hay in 1921. It was undoubtedly moving very slowly. *From the collections of The Henry Ford*

Chapter 5

THE T GOES TRUCKIN'

Stripper chassis, Roadster Pickups, and the TT

It's impossible to think of the Ford Motor Company and not think of trucks. The company's rugged F-Series pickups, which the automaker sells at the rate of approximately one million per year, have been a staple of America's work life and personal transportation for more than half a century.

The F-Series bloodline stretches back directly to the 1925 Model T Roadster Pickup, Ford's first factory-built pickup. Long before then, the Model T provided the basis for commercial vehicles that delivered maximum utility and value.

Underpinning the T's evolution into a haulin' machine was its chassis. With stout side rails, sturdy stamped-steel crossmembers, forged-steel body mounts, and a tough forged vanadium-steel front axle, the Model T car chassis was simple, strong, and lightweight for its size. Additionally, Ford's novel three-point suspension effectively isolated the frame (and powertrain) from much of the road shock that would cause the chassis of less thoughtfully designed vehicles to flex, particularly under load.

Soon after the T's introduction in late 1908, businesses and farmers began requesting a commercial version in letters to dealers and to Henry Ford himself. To meet their needs, in 1911 the Highland Park plant began producing what was listed on Ford's production ledgers as the Commercial Chassis. This was literally a "stripper" T devoid of any bodywork except the cowl, engine cover, radiator, front fenders, and headlamps.

Ford's Commercial Chassis, first offered in 1911 but not officially catalogued until 1914, was essentially a Touring stripped of all bodywork except the cowl, engine cover, radiator, front fenders, and headlamps. Assembled without windshield or seat, the chassis rolled off the Highland Park line with only a wooden bench for a driver's perch. Buyers took their chassis to any number of independent body makers. This factory photo is from 1917. *From the collections of The Henry Ford*

The chassis was assembled without windshield or seat, and to enable it to be driven away, Ford fitted a simple wooden bench straddling the fuel tank. Customers picked up their new T chassis and took it to the independent bodyworks of their choice.

Wood was the primary structural material used for cabs and bodies in those days, and it was used in the numerous body types fitted to Model T over the years, including flatbeds, cargo vans, open- and closed-cab pickups, and huckster wagons. The latter, with their low-sided cargo areas open on three sides and covered by a roof, were popular for hawking farm produce on neighborhood streets.

The chassis also became widely used for fire department pumper and chemical-hose trucks, police paddy wagons, ambulances (the U.S. Army purchased thousands for World War I), and even light dump trucks. In 1923, the Japanese government bought 800 Model T chassis and installed bus bodies on them for use after a massive earthquake destroyed much of Tokyo's transportation system.

The T chassis also underpinned many depot hacks, which were popular with hotels and lodges for carrying passengers from railroad depots to their destinations. Depot hacks—great-grandfathers of the classic Ford "woody"— were as close to rolling cabinetry as a Model T could be. Their seven-passenger bodies were constructed by independent shops, and the beautiful oak or other hardwoods were often finished only with varnish for weather resistance.

While the chassis first became available in 1911, it was not officially catalogued until 1914. Ford previously stated that use of non-Ford bodies would void its warranty. The

The granddaddy of the panel van was Ford's Delivery Car (also known as the Delivery Wagon), offered only for the 1912 model year. Initially, the bodies came only in red, to go with the year's standard dark-blue fenders and chassis. The custom hardwood body of this beautifully restored example faithfully replicates the style of the originals, right down to its arched-roof "C" cab. *Artemis Images*

year after it went on sale, Ford introduced a purpose-built Model T aimed for delivery use.

The Delivery Car (also known as Delivery Wagon) was a one-year wonder. Introduced in late 1911 for the 1912 model year, it featured a semi-enclosed cargo body with open driver's compartment. There were no doors or side windows. The Delivery Car's roof curved up from behind the driver's head and arched downward toward the top rail of the windshield frame, but it did not mechanically connect with it.

It was initially offered in red paint with the standard 1912 Model T dark blue (almost black) fenders and chassis,

but Ford soon switched to selling the Delivery Car with an unpainted body, leaving the livery up to the customer, who often had its body sides sign-painted and lettered to identify the business.

Although its body type was the precursor to the ubiquitous panel van, the Delivery Car was a poor seller. Production for 1912 lasted only about six months. Although the model was catalogued in 1913, the 513 Delivery Cars sold after October 1, 1912, were leftovers, according to Model T technical expert Bruce McCalley. Nonetheless, the Delivery Car had style; its arched roof decades later lured custom-car builders.

CHEVY AND DODGE BATTLE FORD FOR TRUCK TURF

Chevrolet and the Dodge brothers came out of World War I with their sights set on Ford. In 1918, Chevy's 490 Light Delivery chassis was the marque's first-ever truck model, with wooden cabs and utility bodies fitted by various suppliers. It was rated for a 1,000-pound payload and retailed for $595.

The 490 series was Chevrolet's Model T fighter. Its name was its price, identical to Model T's price, which was General Motors' strategy. The Chevy's introduction forced Henry Ford to further lower his prices.

The two competitors were very closely matched, but the Chevy's specs were slightly superior. Its inline four-cylinder engine displaced 171 ci and produced a claimed 21.7 horsepower (the greater efficiency was likely due to its overhead valves), compared with the flathead Model T's 177.6 ci and 20 horsepower. Wheelbases were 102 inches on the Chevy and 100 inches on the T. Both chassis were rated for a maximum payload of 1,000 pounds.

One feature Chevrolet publicly touted as being better than Ford was its three-speed transmission, a sliding-gear type with conventional clutch and floor shifter used on the 490 car.

The Dodges built their first car in 1914 after ending a long business relationship with Henry Ford in which they supplied components for approximately half a million Model Ts. Late in World War I, they built nearly 20,000 half-ton Dodge chassis sets for the U.S. Army, along with cargo trucks and ambulances.

When the war ended, the Dodges converted their military ambulance into the Screenside Commercial Car, an open-panel truck based on a beefed-up, 114-inch-wheelbase car chassis and capable of carrying a 1,000-pound payload. The Screenside's brawny 212-ci flathead inline four gave 35 horsepower when driving a conventional floor-shifted three-speed. In

Chevrolet introduced its 490 series trucks to compete with the Model T truck following World War I. Nearly identical in size and payload, the GM product boasted an overhead-valve engine with slightly more power and a three-speed gearbox with conventional floor shifter. *GM Media Archives*

1924, the Dodge chassis' wheelbase was increased to 116 inches, well suited to larger commercial bodies.

By mixing and matching chassis, running gear, and bodies, anyone could build a custom Ford truck. Apparently that was the case with this handsome stake-bodied rig, photographed in 1917 somewhere in Asia. The brass-radiator chassis is from 1912–1913 and the vehicle features right-hand drive, but its fenders are post-1916 items. *From the collections of The Henry Ford*

Underpowered Workhorse—the TT

Ford's success with the popular Model T chassis inspired its major U.S. competitors to follow suit. In 1918, Chevrolet and the Dodge brothers fired their own volleys in the emerging light-truck war (see page 126). At the same time Ford introduced a new offering that was, in many ways, a true truck rather than a truck-bodied car.

The One-Ton Truck chassis, also known as the TT (for T Truck), was the company's response to a flood of requests for a vehicle with greater payload capacity. Doubling of the car chassis' payload was accomplished using beefier frame components, a longer wheelbase, heavier springs, and larger wheels (available with either pneumatic tires or, like the big rigs of the day, solid-rubber tires bonded to the rims).

The area where the TT suffered most was its 20-horsepower engine and two-speed planetary transmission, the same as in Model T cars. So Ford equipped the TT with a worm-drive axle, which replaced the car's bevel-drive unit. The TT's axle was available in standard (7.25:1) and special (5.2:1) gearing. When it was asked to haul 1,000-pound loads in the light-commercial chassis, power was marginal. In a TT, it was nonexistent.

The term "home away from home" may have been hatched when the owner of this rolling cottage nailed up its last piece of clapboard in 1917. Center of gravity seems not to have been a factor in the builder's plans—but the truck house slept four comfortably. *From the collections of The Henry Ford*

The U.S. Army contracted Ford to design for mass manufacture a light tank for World War I, but the conflict was over before any of the 3-ton machines powered by twin Model T engines passed the prototype stage. This one, shown under test in Highland Park, mounts a short-barreled 50-mm gun. *From the collections of The Henry Ford*

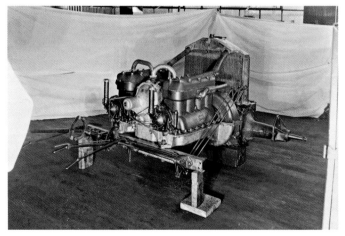

The prototype tank's power module shows its control linkages. Note the oversized cooling system and the large aluminum casting cradling both Model T engines. Even a medium-caliber round fired into the rear of this thin-skinned crawler would have stopped it in its tracks. *From the collections of The Henry Ford*

Frank Morisini remembers working with his father's road-paving company in Pennsylvania as a teenager in the 1930s. "We still operated an old TT dump truck that took all the hell we could give it," he recalled. "We'd load it with hot asphalt but it had no guts, even with a two-speed rear that my father installed when the truck was new.

"Climbing hills took forever in that Ford," he said. "You didn't want to be following us up a long grade on a summer day!"

Accessory catalogs helped give the TT more oomph. One hot item was a Warford three-speed auxiliary transmission, which bolted up behind the stock planetary. The combination gave six forward speeds, enhancing the truck's lugging power.

When one of the popular Ruckstell two-speed, worm-drive rear axles was fitted, the Ford/Warford/Ruckstell drivetrain offered the TT trucker 12 speeds forward—as much torque multiplication as was possible with a paltry 20

Ford produced 5,745 of these ambulance-bodied Model Ts for the Allied forces during World War I. The T proved well-suited to the heavily rutted, muddy terrain of European battlefields. *From the collections of The Henry Ford*

ponies under the hood. Sold through Ford dealers, the Ruckstell axle cost $112 but was reduced to $80 in 1926.

Some TT owners simply yanked out the Ford planetary and installed an aftermarket sliding-gear three- or four-speed main gearbox from Muncie, Jumbo, or another maker. Replacing the T's stock thermo-siphon cooling system with a proper water pump (many kits were available) was another practical modification by TT owners, who regularly stopped on the roadside to wait for their overheated, overloaded engines to cool down.

The TT's production numbers proved its growing popularity. Some 41,000 chassis were built in 1918 (less than

Above: A 1920 TT truck chassis and a Fordson tractor, both fresh off their assembly lines. The Fordson's design and production methods were heavily influenced by the company's experience with the Model T. The crude wooden seat that was fitted atop the truck chassis' fuel tank is missing from this publicity photo. *From the collections of The Henry Ford*

Left: The Smith Form-a-Truck introduced in the late 1910s converted the Model T into a full-fledged 1-ton road tractor. The package included a subframe that strengthened and extended the Ford chassis and provided a trailer pivot. It also came with a chain final-drive gear reduction to make the most of the T's measly 20 horsepower. *From the collections of The Henry Ford*

Ford never officially produced a Coupe Pickup like this one seen at a Colorado vintage-Ford rally, but such a vehicle could easily be assembled from various aftermarket pickup-box conversion kits sold during the 1910s and 1920s. The T owner simply removed the car's turtledeck and bolted on the truck box. *Artemis Images*

one-tenth the Touring car's production, but indicating demand for a work truck). This rose to more than 70,000 in 1919 and nearly doubled to more than 135,000 TTs in 1920. The truck chassis were produced at Highland Park and all 30 U.S. branch plants, as well as at Ford's South American, European, and U.K. facilities.

The volume spurred Ford to introduce its own C-cab body for the TT in early 1924, plus an 8-foot-long express flatbed with or without stakes and canopy. Finally, a complete truck from Ford!

A factory closed-cab TT chassis debuted in April 1925. Ford's letter to its dealers explained that the new all-steel cab was adaptable for use with standard Ford truck bodies, both express and stake types. The cab's doors were extra wide, with plate-glass windows that could be lowered. The upper portion of the hinged windshield swung in or out to provide ventilation. The seat was touted as fitting three people (snugly, at best), and removable panels in the back of the cab permitted access to the cargo body.

continued on page 140

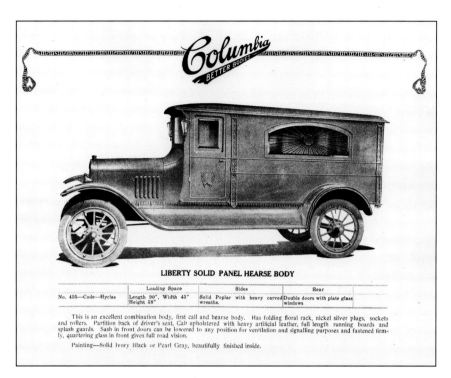

The Columbia Body Company in Detroit was one of many specialist body makers that focused on specific Model T applications, in this case hearses and ambulances. This 1922 Liberty body was crafted from solid poplar. *From the collections of The Henry Ford*

LIBERTY SOLID PANEL HEARSE BODY

	Loading Space	Sides	Rear
No. 455—Code—Hyclas	Length 90", Width 43" Height 58"	Solid Poplar with heavy carved wreaths.	Double doors with plate glass windows

This is an excellent combination body, first call and hearse body. Has folding floral rack, nickel silver plugs, sockets and rollers. Partition back of driver's seat, Cab upholstered with heavy artificial leather, full length running boards and splash guards. Sash in front doors can be lowered to any position for ventilation and signalling purposes and fastened firmly, quartering glass in front gives full road vision.

Painting—Solid Ivory Black or Pearl Gray, beautifully finished inside.

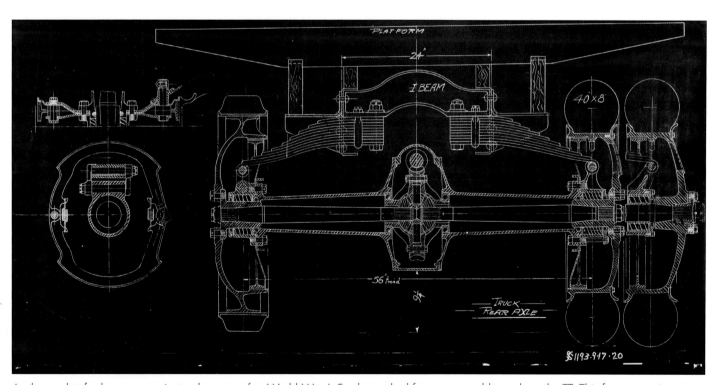

As the market for larger-capacity trucks grew after World War I, Ford searched for ways to add muscle to the TT. This factory engineering drawing dated September 17, 1920, shows an experimental 4-ton drive axle set up for "dually" rear wheels. Also visible is the TT's standard worm-drive differential that limited top speed (unladen) to about 25 miles per hour but gave the 20-horsepower engine all the torque multiplication it could get. *From the collections of The Henry Ford*

Model T–based fire equipment was popular throughout the T's era. Smaller fire departments, in particular, appreciated the Ford chassis' reasonable purchase price, easy maintenance, and low operating costs. This chemical truck, still on active duty in 1932 when this photo was taken, carried a short extension ladder in addition to a quartet of brass dry-chemical tanks on its running board. *From the collections of The Henry Ford*

With help from the local chapter of the Model A Ford Club, volunteers at the Central Ohio Fire Museum in Columbus lovingly restored this 1915 LaFrance–bodied Model T to full operational condition. The gleaming rig now leads a pampered life in parades and antique-vehicle shows. It is equipped with twin 25-gallon chemical tanks mounted across the center of the body. *Author photo*

A business-end view of the Central Ohio Fire Museum's 1915 T reveals 1,000 feet of 2 1/2-inch hose packed neatly in the bed. According to the museum's vintage-truck expert, Bill Hall, LaFrance built 350 chemical-body conversions for Model T commercial chassis and cars between 1915 and 1919. Rear fenders originally from a depot hack–bodied T were used to complete this stunning restoration. *Author photo*

A wintertime delivery of Velvet Brand ice cream ("The Choice of a Million") shows the Detroit Creamery Company's recently purchased 1923 Model T express truck in its element. Curbside delivery drivers in the upper Midwest appreciated even the minimal warmth provided by the optional rollup side curtains and rear enclosure, both of which could easily be removed from the cab during summertime operation. *From the collections of The Henry Ford*

You could say Bruce Wigle was a plumber "flush" with Fords. His impressive fleet, seen here about to begin a major job in 1924, included at least five custom van–bodied TTs, two pickups, and a roadster, at far right. Most of the vehicles are equipped with external racks for carrying long lengths of pipe and tubing. *From the collections of The Henry Ford*

This telephone utilities repair truck is how people all over the United States frequently saw the Ford TT during the 1920s and '30s—looking well-worn and crammed with enough ladders, electrical wire, equipment, and tools to keep a crew of linemen on the job for days. *From the collections of The Henry Ford*

Don Smith of Milan, Michigan, has owned this 1925 station wagon for more than a quarter-century and he drives it regularly in all but the coldest months. Also known as a "suburban" or "depot hack," these earliest Ford "woodies" were often purchased by exclusive hotels and spas in rural vacation spots that used them to transport their well-heeled guests to and from the railroad station. *Author photo*

The handsome body of Don Smith's "hack" is constructed of oak, birch, and maple, and was made by the Buffalo Body Company in New York, one of many suppliers of Ford's station wagon bodies. Smith's car is equipped with rollup side curtains and an aftermarket water pump, which has provided his T-loving family with extra cooling insurance during their long-distance summer trips. Note the accordian-style period luggage rack on the running board. *Author photo*

Standard wooden-spoke artillery wheels fitted with demountable rims and 4.50x21-inch balloon tires grace the rear of Don Smith's depot hack. "A sense of humor and a heck of a lot of work" are the keys to keeping the hardwood-bodied Ts in top condition, says Smith. *Author photo*

In 1925 coal was still a primary source of heat for residential and commercial buildings, so what better way to preach the Ford truck gospel than through the coal-delivery business? Express-bodied TTs used in many vocations were a common sight in American towns through the 1930s. *From the collections of The Henry Ford*

Ford
One Ton Truck
with Closed Cab and
Express Body

The Better Way

The accepted economy of the Ford ton truck is not the only reason why coal dealers prefer this delivery unit.

E. R. Wade, owner and manager of the Acme Coal Co. of Oklahoma City, Okla., says:

"Our experience has shown us two important features of the Ford ton trucks. They are easiest to handle in traffic and there are always men available who can operate Ford trucks satisfactorily."

Flexibility as applied to coal delivery service is essential. This calls for a sufficient number of delivery units to readily serve a wide spread clientele, within a short period of time. A fleet of Ford ton trucks meets this requirement without a large investment.

Your nearest authorized Ford dealer has much information on the subject of better and quicker coal deliveries.

Ford Motor Company
Detroit, Michigan

CARS · TRUCKS · TRACTORS

Ford

continued from page 132

When Model T received its restyle in 1926–1927, the TT did not follow, keeping its circa-1925 front-end look. Ford historians have found evidence of a prototype TT with updated sheet metal, but it did not reach production.

Enter the Roadster Pickup

With the TT established in the one-ton arena, it was time for a complete factory-built light-duty pickup. The announcement came in a Ford Motor Company "factory letter" datelined April 15, 1925, sent from the Chicago branch:

In 1925, Ford Airport was located adjacent to what is now Greenfield Village, on the same large parcel of land that today is occupied by Ford Motor Company's Dearborn Proving Grounds. To draw attention to its Air Transportation Service ground fleet and impress dignitaries using the airport, the automaker built this crown jewel of a TT cargo carrier. Its disc wheels and stainless-steel bodywork were kept polished to a sheen that was likely seen by passengers in the Ford Tri-motor aircraft passing overhead a few years later. *From the collections of The Henry Ford*

As a delivery unit to meet requirements for equipment lighter than that of a one-ton truck, The Ford Motor Company has just added a pick-up body to its commercial car line.

The new body is designed for use on the Ford Runabout, taking the place of the rear deck, and is well adapted to all kinds of light hauling and quick delivery. The Runabout seat affords comfortable riding for the driver and there is ample room for another passenger.

Full protection against inclement weather is provided by the top and side curtains.

The new body is of all steel construction and sturdily built. It is 3 feet, 4 3/4 inches wide and 4 feet, 8 inches long. Sides are 13 inches deep to the flare, so that loading space is sufficient to meet all demands of light delivery. The end gate is the same as that on the Express type body of the one-ton truck and when partially lowered is securely held in place by chains.

The brute of the Greenfield Village Model T fleet is this 1921 TT wrecker. Although not as visible to the public as the Village's passenger-carrying Tourings, the brawny TT is always ready behind the scenes whenever muscle is needed. *Author photo*

The 1925 Roadster Pickup is among the rarest of all Model T body configurations. It combined the standard Roadster body tub with a factory-installed pickup box in place of the car's turtledeck rear compartment. The pickup model was offered for only a few months in 1925, prior to introduction of the restyled 1926 Ts.

Officially catalogued as the "Model T Runabout with Pickup Body," it was priced at $281 FOB Detroit—$21 more than the standard T roadster. The little truck was the next logical step beyond offering the separate pickup box as a stand-alone option ($25), which the company had been doing since December 1924.

The Roadster Pickup turned out to be a fairly popular model its first year, with nearly 34,000 sold. For 1926, it gained the T's new front-end sheet metal, a new cargo box

with revised mounting for the rear fenders, and a metal panel that gave access to the battery located underneath the front end of the box.

In 1926, the pickup's price jumped to $366, reflecting additional equipment that was either optional or unavailable on the 1925 model. The list of options included an electric starter, battery, and demountable tires. Balloon tires were available for $15.

Factory-made pickups were painted Commercial Green in 1927 (radiator shells were black), but if the pickup box was ordered separately, it also wore black. Production records show that, including the separate pickup boxes, Ford produced more than 75,000 pickups in 1926 and approximately 28,000 in 1927 before the Model T lines were shut down permanently.

Model T experts believe this stake-bodied TT, photographed in April 1926, may have been a prototype for an improved TT that never debuted due to the car being taken out of production in 1927. As the Model T became obsolete, so too did the TT, particularly in the critical areas of power, payload, and driver comfort. Rear tires on this truck are 5x20-inch. *From the collections of The Henry Ford*

A nicely restored 1926–1927 pickup cruises Main Street during a vintage-Ford rally. During the T's last model years, the pickup box was still available as a stand-alone accessory from Ford dealers, for conversion of Roadsters to pickups. During 1926 Ford made the important switch from enamel paints to the new faster-drying Pyroxylin lacquers and reintroduced color in its vehicles. *Artemis Images*

Barney Navarro was an early speed-equipment innovator and manufacturer who made his name going fast on the dry lakes in modified Model Ts. After World War II, Navarro built this supercharged Ford V-8-powered T roadster that ran nearly 147 miles per hour. *Greg Sharp/NHRA Wally Parks Motorsports Museum*

Chapter 6

RACING AND RODDING THE T

A century of going fast—and keeping "cool"

The car that put the world on wheels had a top speed of about 40 miles per hour, with a tailwind. But despite its humble roots, the Model T became the bedrock of automobile racing in America.

Name the speed contest and the T has been there and done it. In countless events, the gutsy little Ford performed so well that it made competitors crazy and fans delirious.

The Model T and its infinite racing iterations have toppled records and copped winners' trophies on dirt tracks, board tracks, dry lakes, and salt flats. They've beaten all comers to the top of Pikes Peak and crossed the Indianapolis finish line ahead of much costlier and more glamorous Mercedes, Bugattis, Millers, and Duesenbergs. They've charged 2,000 miles across the Mexican desert in the Carrera Panamericana road race and dominated the drag strip quarter-mile.

It was in Model T–based cars that scores of race drivers got their start. T racing, during their teenage years, also helped propel motorsports titans Bill France Sr. and Wally Parks, founders of NASCAR and the National Hot Rod Association (NHRA), respectively, into their famous careers.

HOT ROD OF THE MONTH

Sitting in the driver's seat is Eddie Hulse, who, a few moments after this picture was taken, drove number 668, to set a new SCTA record for Class C roadsters. Hulse, a native Californian, nosed out Randy Shinn, a long-time top honor holder for the RC Class. Shinn's old record was 129.40 in a channeled Mercury T.

Keeping the Car Out Front by George Riley—Page 10

The ingenuity of American racers and rodders transformed underpowered, ungainly Model Ts into impressive speed machines of all types. A modified T was the natural choice for the cover of the inaugural 1948 issue of *Hot Rod* magazine. Eddie Hulse's dry lakes racer wears a sleek "track" nose, and its Runabout body tub is channeled to sit low on the frame rails. *Ken Gross archive*

Even European racers embraced the flyin' flivver. In 1923, a modified Model T finished 14th in the inaugural 24 Hours of Le Mans. Like most T racers, the car was a bit of a *metisse* (mongrel)—its Montier overhead-valve (OHV) cylinder head and its four-speed transmission both were French-made.

Throughout the past century, the T's snug Roadster and Touring bodies have been wedded to all types of powertrains, from the simple OHV conversions offered as Ford hop-up equipment in the 1920s to the 2,000-horsepower nitro-

burning V-8s of the modern era. In the hands of Norm Grabowski, Ed "Big Daddy" Roth, Tommy Ivo, and other creative geniuses in the 1960s, the T served as a blank canvas for many landmark hot rods.

Indeed, the eminently affordable Model T is the grand-daddy of hot rods and hot rodding, and it's directly responsible for the birth of the American speed shop. Not only did the homebuilt T speedster craze prior to World War I spark interest in the car as a competitive dirt-track tool, but it also spawned the aftermarket speed-equipment industry that is a multibillion-dollar colossus today.

Remarkably, a new wave of speedster mania is inspiring twenty-first-century "T heads" who love building, tuning, and tweaking the racy relics. And an appreciation for well-executed T-buckets continues unabated in the hot rod community.

Henry Ford and his small team of draftsmen never could have dreamed that Tin Lizzie would have so much game!

Epic Coast-to-Coast Victory

In the early days, Fords were "the bread-and-butter of the racing industry before it was really an industry," observed Leo Levine, author of *Ford: The Dust and the Glory*, the milestone two-volume chronicle of the company's racing history.

Levine rated the stone-simple and extremely under-stressed T engine as one of the three most important production-car engines (along with Ford's 1932 flathead V-8 and the 1955 Chevrolet V-8) used in American racing in the twentieth century. He noted that for four decades, the 176.7-ci long-stroke four was used to power a plethora of sporting machinery, giving "every kid working on a shoestring the chance to be a racer."

Henry Ford did not aspire to be a racecar maker, but he did see the value of limited racing and record-setting to help sell his cars. When the Model T was still in its first year of production, Ford bet on the new car's reputation, and that of his company, by entering two "factory" cars in the first auto race across the United States.

The challenge of a coast-to-coast race was laid down by millionaire Robert Guggenheim in the spring of 1909. Guggenheim, who made his fortune in mining, conceived the race to promote the Alaskan Yukon Pacific Exposition slated to open in Seattle on June 1, 1909. The contest was billed as the Ocean-to-Ocean Automobile Endurance Contest, with a $3,500 trophy and $2,000 cash for the winner.

Ford's two-car team charges west during the 1909 New York-to-Seattle Ocean-to-Ocean Automobile Endurance Contest. The factory-prepared Ts weighed 950 pounds each, but the lack of weather protection meant a punishing journey for co-drivers Frank Kulick and H. B. Harper (No. 1 car, at right) and the winning No. 2 car of Bert Scott and Jimmy Smith. Note the Touring that has pulled out to follow the racecars. *From the collections of The Henry Ford*

The awards were peanuts compared with the risk, however. A poor showing or outright failure could doom any fledgling marque in those early days of the auto industry. But the confident Ford intended to silence critics who said his lightweight car was too fragile and that his company couldn't survive on one car model alone.

The Ocean-to-Ocean race was big news in America. President William Howard Taft had agreed to open the exposition by pressing a golden telegraph key in the White House. The President's key would simultaneously send a signal to New York Mayor George McClellan, son of the Civil War Union general. Upon hearing the signal, McClellan would then fire a gold-plated pistol to start the race.

At the time, more than 200 companies were calling themselves "automobile manufacturers" in the United States, and 36 of them, including Ford, boldly accepted Guggenheim's cross-country challenge. However, the initial list of entrants quickly shrank to 14, then finally to just 5, as company leaders weighed their cars' chances in what would clearly be a grueling test.

Locals examine the victorious No. 2 Ford mired in Great Plains mud during its return trip from Seattle. Such conditions were typical in the 1909 Ocean-to-Ocean race, but the tractability of the Model Ts overcame all odds. *From the collections of The Henry Ford*

Those who bailed out gave Guggenheim plenty of excuses. Some objected to the initial set of rules, claiming the race would encourage speed-law violations. Others whined that it would not be a true endurance contest, since the initial rules permitted swapping engines and other key parts along the route.

But Henry Ford didn't flinch. Putting his young company's reputation squarely on the line, Ford publicly announced that he would enter his cars even if the rules did not allow repairs. "The Ford will stay in, even if they prohibit tire replacements or spark plug renewals," promised *Ford Times*, the company's in-house magazine.

Rather than encourage an all-out speed race, the finalized rules set a point-to-point route schedule by the day and hour. They also prohibited replacement of the engine crankcase, cylinders, transmission case, steering gear, frame, and axles. To keep the entrants honest, all original parts were stamped by the American Automobile Club's technical committee.

As the June 1 starting date approached, the organizers tried various tactics to attract more auto companies to race against the already hot-selling Model T. When the deadline arrived, however, only six cars were on the final entrants' list. Two of them were standard 22-horsepower Ford Touring models.

Stripped of their fenders and rear bodywork, the Ts became trim, 950-pound two-seaters. Completely open, without tops or weather protection, they promised to be a punishing test of driver stamina.

The No. 1 car was co-driven by Frank Kulick and H. B. Harper, editor of *Ford Times*. Kulick was one of Henry Ford's first five employees and the company's resident hot-shoe for many years. The No. 2 car was piloted by Bert Scott and Jimmy Smith.

Winning the Ocean-to-Ocean race gave Henry Ford national publicity and helped boost the new Model T's reputation at a time when many critics considered the car too spindly to hold up under hard use. *From the collections of The Henry Ford*

Facing the pair of Fords were four large cars: a six-cylinder Acme and three big four-cylinder autos made by Stearns, Shawmut, and Itala (the only foreign entry). Each competitor had more than twice the Model T's horsepower, but they were also at least three times as heavy as the Fords, giving the lightweight Ts a superior power-to-weight ratio.

Henry Ford even supplied a pace car, one of his six-cylinder Model K-640 Runabouts, for the New York–St. Louis section of the race.

At 3:30 p.m. on June 1, President Taft pushed the telegraph key, Mayor McClellan pulled the golden pistol's trigger from the steps of City Hall, and five cars were off in a plume of smoke (the Stearns had engine trouble and started the race four days later). Ahead of the racers were more than 4,000 miles of mostly rudimentary byways, wagon trails, old Indian paths, and wilderness.

Checkpoints were set up in pre-selected towns, but west of the Mississippi River the going got really tough. Kansas had approximately 275 miles of what were loosely known as "improved" roads, which typically meant the ruts were less than 4 inches deep! Colorado had 200 miles of the same. Washington was better off; it had 2,000 miles of improved roads, thanks to its active automobile club.

As the Fords pressed on, Seattle must have seemed as far away as the moon. Jimmy Smith, the mechanic of the No. 2 car, logged in his diary:

There are no roads west of St. Louis, just mud. No paved roads. When it was dry, it wasn't bad. I had to push the car along when it was wet. Out west there were sand beds. When it rained, it flooded up about a foot-and-a-half to two-feet deep. Wade through it first, then pull the car through. Then we would dry out the [ignition] coils and go on.

At a point in Kansas on June 8, after miles of slogging through muddy roads and soaked by constant rain, Kulick and Harper decided to stop for the night. Smith and Scott in the No. 2 car soldiered on. Within a few miles they skidded off the road and into a stream. They had to wait until the next morning for their teammates to come along and pull them out. Then they noticed the front axle was bent.

"We found we were right near a railroad," Smith told Leo Levine years later. "So we got the section gang there and straightened the axle again. We got back in and away we went. We didn't know where we were—that is, know where the others were."

By the time the Fords reached Denver on June 12, they were in the lead. The Stearns, having started four days behind the others, was out of the hunt. The Itala had been damaged by a freight train while crossing a rail trestle. The Acme had dropped back after crashing twice. And the once-leading Shawmut was delayed after getting stuck in quicksand. (The same fate had befallen the Fords, but the lightweight Model Ts proved easy to extricate. The drivers levered them out of the deep muck using the roof of an abandoned pig pen.)

Over the next five days, though, the impressively reliable Shawmut turned up the wick. It swapped the lead with the Fords as T No. 1 suffered a broken wheel and the No. 2 car again broke its axle. Repairs made, on June 16 in Wyoming the T teams chose to split up as they sparred with the Shawmut toward Seattle.

Through ruggedly beautiful Idaho and Washington, the Fords remained within hours of each other but endured more setbacks. One car ran out of gas. They encountered an obstinate ferryboat operator who refused to carry them across a lake. They had to traverse a snow-choked gorge. And the No. 2 car briefly caught fire during a gas stop.

But on June 23, the No. 2 Smith/Scott Model T was the first car to arrive in Seattle. As the exhausted duo crossed the finish line in the city's fairground in front of 15,000 cheering spectators (including Henry Ford), Guggenheim clicked his stopwatch at 12:55 p.m. The winning car had covered 4,106 miles in 22 days and 55 minutes, at an average speed of 7.75 miles per hour.

The No. 1 Kulick/Harper T entered the fairground two days after the winners, and more than a day behind the second-place Shawmut. The Ford had to be disqualified, however, because Kulick and Harper had replaced an axle broken in the mountains.

The Acme chugged into the city four days later, and the Itala, which had expired in Wyoming, finally rolled into Seattle on a railcar. According to a 1959 recounting of the race in *The Antique Automobile*, protests of alleged rule-breaking by the Fords were filed by representatives of the Acme and Shawmut companies. After hearing their grievances, Guggenheim awarded the trophy and prize money to Model T No. 2.

Not only did Jimmy Smith and Bert Scott successfully complete the first U.S. coast-to-coast race, but they also drove the battered winner back across the country!

"Ford Cars for 1910—Every Car a Duplicate of the New York–Seattle Winner," shouted the full-page advertisement in the August 25, 1909, issue of *The Horseless Age*. The Ford ad was an early example of the old "race on Sunday, sell on Monday" lure and noted that the victorious T was in the process of racking up another 3,000 miles on its return trip to New York. (Well after the race, however, the car was disqualified when it was discovered that its engine had been replaced during the race).

Still, it was proof that the Model T was more than up to the job of taking people anywhere they wanted to go.

T on Ice—107 Miles per Hour

Henry Ford took his latest product racing again in August 1910 when he entered two Model Ts in the first of a new road-race series in Elgin, Illinois. Sponsored by the Elgin Watch Company, the contest was run over an 8 1/2-mile course containing six corners and one hairy rise that sent the cars airborne. The Fords were to be piloted by Frank Kulick and Jim Hatch, but the cars were disqualified before the start of the 16-lap race for weighing less than the minimum 1,400 pounds.

A year later at Elgin, with no minimum-weight restrictions, Kulick and his factory T placed second. He covered

Soon after winning America's first transcontinental race, Henry Ford sought victory at the new 8 1/2-mile road-race circuit in Elgin, Illinois. While the two factory Ts were deemed too light to qualify in 1910, Ford returned to Elgin in 1911. Frank Kulick and riding mechanic Jim Hatch took second place. *From the collections of The Henry Ford*

Ford's *999-II* was a lean, purposeful racecar that embodied the lessons learned from each of Henry Ford's previous competition machines. Today it's on display at The Henry Ford Museum and still looks like it could go 100 miles per hour. *From the collections of The Henry Ford*

the 136 miles in 2 hours, 39 minutes—8 minutes behind the winning Abbott-Detroit. He only stopped once, for a change of tires.

Kulick next went searching for speed records at one of Henry Ford's old haunts: the frozen surface of Lake St. Clair near Detroit. On February 17, 1912, his T racer, dubbed *999-II* in tribute to Henry Ford's second racecar, *999*, established a one-way record for a Ford car of 34.8 seconds (104.45 miles per hour) on the icy mile-long straightaway.

Kulick backed it up with an even quicker 33.4-second/107.78-mile-per-hour run. It was a sensational performance for a factory-tuned Model T in only its third full year of production.

Bobtail Racers

Three keys to making a car go faster are increasing its power, reducing its weight, and improving its aerodynamics. Speed-seeking Model T owners began tackling these changes soon after the flivver was introduced. Little did they know that they were planting the seeds of American hot rodding.

The first notable appearance of modified T racers was in 1910–1911. To prepare their Fords for the dirt tracks, the early road races at Elgin and Santa Monica, and the board-track motordromes opening up across the United States, the pioneering speed-freaks first stripped the car of all nonessential parts. Fenders, headlamps, the huge upright windshield, and all bodywork aft of the cowl were removed. Next came shortening the stock 100-inch wheelbase by 4 or 5 inches, which helped shed a few more pounds and quickened the steering.

The already-Spartan Ford was thus transformed into a truly skeletal machine, basically a rolling chassis to which a shallow pan with minimal padding was added for a driver's seat. With overbored engines, raised compression, and larger carburetors providing a few more ponies—the big

continued on page 156

A steely-eyed Frank Kulick warms up *999-II* in preparation for his speed runs on frozen Lake St. Clair on February 17, 1912. With tire chains for traction, the T-based racecar set a one-way record of 104.45 miles per hour on the icy mile straightaway, then backed it up with an amazing 107.78-mile-per-hour run. *From the collections of The Henry Ford*

Above: The speedster craze took off soon after the Model T's launch, and it's still big fun within the T hobby today. This pre-1915 example features a handcrafted wooden body, perhaps of tongue-and-groove construction. Its overall shape is inspired by the European racecars of the period. Note the half-round step for easier ingress into the tight cockpit. *From the collections of The Henry Ford*

Make Your Ford a $3,000 Car *from the standpoint of motor service.*

Andrew Rotello, Rockford, Ill., a consistent race winner, in his Laurel equipped Ford, No. 1 on the inside of the track, at the start of the August 28 races in Rockford, where he won three cups in as many starts against a large field of fast cars.

ROOF 16 OVERHEAD VALVE EQUIPMENT
A Power Device Needed by Every Ford Owner

One hundred percent extra efficiency, with greater gasoline and oil economy, for either touring car or truck. Hill climbing for the touring car owner beyond his wildest dreams. Sand, mud, or the steepest grades have no terrors for the Ford owner with the Roof 16 valve cylinder head.

FORD RACING CARS

SPEED—Ford cars with the Roof 16-valve cylinder head equipment have been rivals of the best racing cars on mile and half mile tracks, and have practically driven the high-priced racing cars from competition, excepting on speedways. Joseph C. Hayes, L. E. Kerbs Williams Bros., Ben Lawell, C. F. Goltry, Paul M. Boozer, James C. Hackney, Fatz Willard and hundreds of other famous Ford drivers with speed records of from 75 to 97 miles per hour attest the wonderful power given to a Ford by the use of the Roof 16 overhead valve equipment.

We are headquarters for everything necessary in Ford speed equipment, including polished nickel Roof 16 overhead valve equipment, Aluminite and Triple Lite pistons and rings, gray iron pistons and rings complete, Aluminite and Triple Lite connecting rods, parts for underslinging chassis, nickel steel racing gears three to one ratio, racing carburetors, everything in ignition equipment, counter-balance for crankshafts, high speed camshafts, wire wheels and steering gears.

Tell us what you want. We can supply it. Send for photographs of our beautiful racing bodies and racing radiators, which are our own special design.

Get our special circular on long mileage tires and illustrated folder showing our full line of Special, Touring, Roadster and Racing Bodies for Fords.

DEALERS—GARAGEMEN—REPAIRMEN

The ROOF-PEUGEOT TYPE CYLINDER HEAD FOR FORDS IS AN ALL-YEAR SELLER. THEY ARE QUICKLY AND EASILY INSTALLED—SET RIGHT IN PLACE OF THE OLD CYLINDER HEAD. ROCKER ARMS OPERATE FROM THE REGULAR CAMSHAFT. Every Ford owner is a likely prospect, every Ford truck owner is a SURE SALE. If you want a steady stream of business throughout the year that pays, get our agency terms. Send for free illustrated literature of the greatest selling specialty for 1920. Place one equipment in your territory and it will bring every Ford owner to your door.

COMPLETE EQUIPMENT, NOTHING EXTRA TO BUY. Do not fail to get our prices and our wonderful agency proposition for your territory if not taken. WRITE TODAY.

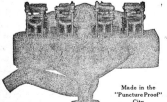

Made in the "Puncture Proof" City

DELIVERY ON
Sixteen Valve Cylinder Heads
for DODGE MOTORS
Will begin after January 1, 1921

LAUREL MOTORS CORPORATION
ANDERSON, INDIANA

Left: When Henry Ford refused to deliver more horsepower to his Model T customers, the aftermarket stepped in. Robert Roof's overhead-valve cylinder-head conversions sold by Laurel Motors were one of the hot setups of the 1920s. The kit was essentially a bolt-on, but despite delivering a meaningful power boost it really didn't turn a T into a "$3,000 car." *Image courtesy Charlie Yapp/Secrets of Speed Society*

Opposite: The popular Rajo heads for Fords came in a variety of valvetrain configurations. They were advertised as benefiting both power and fuel efficiency, but most customers bought them for their speed-enhancing capabilities. *Image courtesy Charlie Yapp/Secrets of Speed Society*

**Quicker, easier starting in the coldest weather.
Instant pick-up and remarkable flexibility—from
5 to 50 miles per hour in less than two city blocks.
More miles per gallon — from 20 to 30 average.
Power to pull through all roads — double that of
the standard Ford engine. And more speed than
you'll ever need — from 5 to 70 miles per hour in
high with the standard gear ratio! . . . . . This is
what you get with the big, specially designed carburetor; hot spot, intake manifold and the eight
over-size overhead valves of the Rajo Model "B"
. . . Your Ford, super-powered with a Model "B"
Rajo Valve-in-Head, will give you the smoothest
operating, most flexible, highest powered, speed-
iest car on the road. . . . Three Rajo models give
you a wide choice. A post card will bring you full
details of the complete Rajo line. Write today.**

DEALERS: *The Rajo dealership assures you a three-way
profit — a profit on the sale — a profit on
the installation—a profit on the service. Write for the facts.*

Rajo Motor Company, 1354 Racine St., Racine, Wisconsin

continued from page 152

bag of speed tricks was yet to come—these naked T racers were known as "bobtails" and "go-jobs." They were ancestors of the original hot rods that emerged in the 1930s.

Ed Winfield, one of the first big names in the speed-equipment business, was 14 years old when he built a bobtail T in 1910. After World War I, he became famous by offering his own Winfield carburetors, camshafts, and racing cylinder heads for the four-cylinder Fords.

From the minimalist bobtails came the next step in the Model T's performance evolution. By 1914–1915 a cottage industry had emerged to support the skyrocketing popularity of racing Fords. Small manufacturers and machine shops began offering streamlined racecar bodies (single- or two-seaters), higher-ratio differential gears, ignition distributors to replace the flywheel magneto, aluminum pistons, demountable wire-spoked wheels, and various other components. All were aimed at "hopping up" the little four-bangers to a level far exceeding anything from Highland Park.

The racing bodies made by Morton and Brett, Paco, Champion, and others emulated the sleek European Grand Prix cars of the period. They quickly became the look for the Ford-based machines that thundered around the hardwood ovals. As *The Automobile* revealed in its September 14, 1916, report on the latest racecar technology seen at Chicago Speedway, the Fords reflected both the creativity of their builders and the greater mix of speed parts entering the market:

> *The car which bore No. 37, built and driven by B. F. Davis of Paris, Ill., is a typical representative of how a Ford motor may be coupled with hybrid parts to make a car which is capable of close to 70 miles per hour. Davis won the 30-mile Illinois State Championship, but unfortunately broke a rod in the free-for-all when he was running close second to Paul Harvey [a leading Ford racer].*
>
> *The motor is a Ford. The bore is the same as the stroke. Valves were enlarged to 1 5/8 in., Rich tungstens being used. The carburetor is a Master and the magneto a Bosch. The camshaft was not altered. A Monroe frame is used to undersling a Scripps-Booth axle on the front and a combination Ford and Scripps-Booth axle on the rear. This combination includes a Ford differential and housing with a Scripps-Booth floating axle. The high*

Champion radiator and formidable-looking streamline body gave the car a full-fledged racing appearance.

Crazy for Speedsters

Who wouldn't love to have that racing appearance in a daily driver? Ford's track successes begot the Model T Speedster, an aftermarket body conversion that enabled enthusiasts to transform their stodgy flivvers into stylishly sporty cars for relatively low cost. Speedster mania started in the mid-teens and continued through the 1920s. Many Model T fans say it never really ended (more on that later in this chapter).

Some speedsters were homebuilt. The owners removed the car's stock body and then formed their own out of sheet metal or even wood. The cottage industry also jumped in with gusto. At least two dozen companies advertised steel speedster bodies in the auto magazines. Many of them were designed to fit the stock T frame using the same attachment points.

Advice for converting a Model T was widely circulated in the popular press. *Dyke's Automobile and Gasoline Engine*

Model T speedsters became a thriving business in the years before World War I and even spread across the Atlantic. This pith-helmeted Dutch enthusiast is preparing to take his low-and-lovely Tempo Sport–bodied T for a canter in 1911. The Tempo bodies were made in The Netherlands. *From the collections of The Henry Ford*

The long list of U.S. companies offering speedster body kits for road and racing use included Bub, Mercury, Paco, Laurel Motors, Faultless, Hine-Watt, Maxwell, Morton & Brett, Champion Racing Body Co., O. T. Ford Speed and Power Equipment Mfg., Cyclone, Greyhound and F. M. Ames (seen here). *Catalog image courtesy Charlie Yapp/Secrets of Speed Society*

Encyclopedia, the bible of automotive knowledge, included a special section devoted mainly to speedster building.

"For Fords the combinations offered by concerns making a business of this kind of work are indeed attractive," noted *Dyke's*. "You can get a complete outfit of radiator, hood, floor boards, rear gasoline tank, and body in the neighborhood of $100, and it is surprising what a difference these make."

Most of the kits also came with two bucket seats. Few included any sort of windscreen to deflect bugs away from the driver's teeth—the stock Ford "barn door" windshield was sacrificed to the gods of speed.

The *Dyke's* editor explained that he had helped build several Model T speedsters that turned out "exceptionally fast" for the money invested. He concluded that with a little ingenuity "quite a presentable racy roadster can result from combinations with old chassis."

The long, swooping fenders and rounded noses of many Speedster kits gave the cars a lean, graceful flair reminiscent of Mercer Raceabouts and Stutz Bearcats, America's first true sports cars.

"A body of this design lightens the burden on the engine and consequently means more speed and less cost of operation," claimed a 1916 ad for the Cyclone Speedster body ($68.75 in primer, or $78.75 painted in a choice of red, yellow, blue, or black).

"It is all the craze now to fit out your Ford in speed style," the ad continued, "and it is really a good thing, on account of the added pleasure of travelling faster, the saving in tires and gasoline, and the different appearance it gives your car."

Speedster bodies generally weighed 225–250 pounds, depending on equipment. Because they were lighter than the stock body, owners could remove one leaf from each of the car's springs, which lowered the vehicle and improved its aerodynamics.

"A Ford Speedster with a hopped-up engine was a pretty fast car," recalled Dean Batchelor in his milestone 1995 book, *The American Hot Rod*. "Many of them were able to top 100 mph which, in the 1920s, was a tremendous feat."

Speedster engines ranged from mild to wild when Model Ts were the "everyman's" racecar. Today's tuners have 100 years of accumulated knowledge and can select from catalogs full of upgraded components. The mill in Sarah Zimmer's car, built in 2006, gets its juice from a modern alternator and coil-and-distributor ignition. But the real tricks lurk within the cast iron. *David LaChance/Hemmings Classic Car*

In today's vintage racing scene, it's not uncommon to see T speedsters showing their tails to purpose-built sportscars—in this case, a BMW 328—during the Pittsburgh Vintage GP at Schenley Park. Miles Whitlock's blue beauty is based on a 1919 chassis, with its front leaf spring inverted to lower the car 4 inches. Its handsome bodywork boasts aluminum panels over a wooden structure. *Walter Pietrowicz/september8th.com*

A 2.0-liter version of Henry Ford's cast-iron motor powers Whitlock's speedster, inhaling through a single updraft carburetor controlled by the classic Model T hand throttle on the steering column. The car's two-speed transmission is also stock T, its brake band fortified with a Kevlar lining. Whitlock reckons the speedster is good for 60 miles per hour on a long straight. *Walter Pietrowicz/september8th.com*

Model T engines, running gear, and bodies formed the backbone of American dirt-track racing for decades. "Track Ts" such as this restored example from the 1940s were light, cheap to build, and regularly won on the short tracks. Bill France Sr., Wilbur Shaw, Troy Ruttman, and other circle-track greats got their start in Model T racers. *Dain Gingerelli*

Frontys Rule the Roaring Twenties

Dirt-track racing and Fords went together like baseball and Babe Ruth in the 1920s. The sport's popularity exploded immediately after World War I, and within the next decade there were approximately 1,000 dirt tracks across the United States and Canada. Many of them had been purpose-built for auto racing.

American circle-track racing has always been pure excitement—grids full of bellowing single-seaters battling wheel-to-wheel with constant passing and powersliding. The fans flocking to the half-mile and mile ovals loved the action, and the ubiquitous Model T was its backbone for three decades.

The widely available Ford provided excellent feedstock for a competitive half-mile racecar. But the long-stroke flathead four was no powerhouse. With a three-bearing crankshaft, Babbitt bearings, and splash lubrication, it was not designed for sustained high-rpm racing.

Enter Chevrolet—Louis and Gaston, that is. After selling his share of the eponymous company he formed with William Durant in 1915, Louis, along with his brother Gaston, founded the Frontenac Motor Corporation in Indianapolis to build top-shelf racecars. The "Frontys" had some successes, but the company struggled financially.

The brothers ultimately planned to launch a new road car, but they needed capital to do it. So they decided to finance the project by making speed equipment for Model T Fords. In doing so, they became the premier T race tuners of the 1920s.

The Frontenac-Ford OHV and overhead-cam (OHC) cylinder-head conversions were the brothers' most famous product (see pages 160–161). Additionally, the company sold complete Ford-powered turn-key racecars with chassis specially set up for the dirt, board tracks, or pavement.

continued on page 162

HEAD GAMES
Fortifying Fords with OHV and OHC power

When early racers turned to Ford's cheap and plentiful Model T, one of their goals was to improve its ability to breathe.

High-performance engines pack a big gulp of air and fuel into their cylinders, then exhale the combustion gases quickly and completely. But the T was built for slow, not for go. With a low compression ratio, small valves located in the cylinder block, a meager 1,800-rpm power peak, and other limitations, the Ford was not a deep-breather.

Developments in Europe soon influenced American thinking and gave the T a lot more punch. In 1913, French engineer Ernst Henri dazzled the world with his revolutionary Peugeot racing engines featuring DOHC and four valves per cylinder. Around the same time, Mercedes debuted a high-speed, SOHC engine designed by Wilhelm Maybach. Both units became instant benchmarks, and discussion of their merits extended to the United States, where a few forward thinkers already recognized the benefits of putting an engine's valves upstairs in the cylinder head rather than in the block.

It's not clear who was first to introduce an OHV head for Fords, but by the mid-1920s many companies had jumped into the field. Robert Roof's 16-valve head featuring pushrod-actuated rocker arms was developed during World War I. By 1918 he was marketing it as the "Peugeot-type head for Fords" through the Laurel Motors Corporation of Anderson, Indiana. List price: $100.

Roof was a major innovator in Model T hop-up equipment, and his competitors in the OHV head game (in terms of numbers produced) were Frontenac and Rajo, according to Charlie Yapp, whose Secrets of Speed Society caters to vintage high-performance four-cylinder Fords.

The name Rajo was an abbreviation combining the name of the Wisconsin city where the heads were made, Racine, and the first name of their creator, Joe Jagersberger. Many others also produced hot heads for Ts, notably Craig-Hunt and Morton and Brett (both based in Indianapolis), Gallivan, Joe Gemsa, McDowell, Riley, and Akron, to name just a few.

Some of the heads used pushrods to actuate their valves. Others employed either an SOHC or DOHC. A few oddballs were F-head types that put the intake valves in the head and used the valves in the block for exhaust. There were also 8-valve and 16-valve heads, with various port configurations and carburetor mounting schemes.

Prices in the mid-1920s typically ranged from approximately $100 to around $750 (for the sophisticated Gallivan gear-driven DOHC head), according to Jack Fox's The Illustrated History of Sprint Car Racing: 1896–1942. By comparison, the median price of a new home in the United States at the time was about $5,500. But the results often justified the cost.

Niles Gary learned the value of his Gallivan-equipped T after running the straightaway mile on the Wildwood, New Jersey, beach in 30 seconds flat (120 miles per hour) in August 1926. Dutch Baumann undoubtedly felt his Fronty-Ford was a good value when he won 43 firsts out of 52 starts in Midwest dirt-track events during 1928.

For sheer numbers and their Indy 500 competition history, the Frontenac heads are the best known of all the Model T conversions. The Chevrolet brothers' shop in Indianapolis offered three different Frontenac heads for T engines. The Model R and S-R heads, designed by ex-Duesenberg engineer Cornelius van Ranst, were pushrod OHV types. The S-R had two spark plugs per cylinder and dual carburetors. Frontenac also made upgrade kits for the R and S-R heads that converted them to a chain-driven SOHC configuration.

Frontenac's crowning glory was the Model D-O head, designed by James Sakayama, a Japanese-American. D-O designated DOHC (chain driven). With four 1.93-inch valves per cylinder set at a 60-degree included angle, it gave optimum breathing potential.

The Ford head business provided much-needed cash flow to the struggling Frontenac Motor Corporation during its financial crisis in 1922. While various histories have repeated Frontenac's claim of producing more than 10,000 heads (60 per day!) during the early 1920s, such numbers today are disputed as wildly optimistic according to many Model T and vintage Ford racing experts. Nonetheless, it is safe to say the Fronty heads were one of the most popular pieces of speed equipment sold for any car during the 1920s.

Of course, the capability of any Model T engine fitted with an OHV or OHC head ultimately depended on a host of other modifications to the base engine to make it sufficiently robust for racing. But the Fronty, Rajo, Roof, and other heads helped put Fords in countless winner's circles for many years.

Frontenac overhead-valve "R" cylinder heads were in big demand during the T's racing heyday. This restored example, with Warford gearbox, is one of a fantastic collection of high-performance T engines and speed equipment on display at Bill Smith's Museum of American Speed in Lincoln, Nebraska. *Image courtesy Bill Smith*

continued from page 159

The Fronty-Fords, as the cars were nicknamed, came in different flavors. They could be built to order, or buyers could choose from three standard models: the $1,850 Model 214 equipped with the R cylinder head; the $2,000 Model 214A with the S-R head; and the Model 214B fitted with the whiz-bang D-O head and priced at $2,300 (in 1923). The cars were offered with a choice of running gear. Initially, the Fronty racing bodies were sourced from Morton and Brett, but later other makes were available.

Weighing 1,350 pounds and geared down to a maximum speed of 70 miles per hour, the Fronty-Fords were highly competitive on half-mile ovals and short courses, regularly beating much more expensive opposition. On longer courses, a dual overhead cam (DOHC) Fronty-Ford could be geared to exceed 110 miles per hour—blindingly quick for a Model T–based machine but outclassed by the 130-mile-per-hour Millers and Duesenbergs.

However, T-based racers regularly held their own against the exotica and often headed them past the checkers. On October 31, 1925, Sam Ross and his Fronty-Ford defeated four Millers and a pair of Duesies in the 100-mile race in Detroit. On the same date, Wilbur Shaw put his 16-valve Fronty-Ford into the winner's circle at the 1-mile Hawthorne Speedway near Chicago. He averaged 74 miles per hour for the 100-mile race.

Even though some considered the Fronty-Fords not fast enough for the longer board tracks, Jack Curtner took his to the 1 1/8-mile wooden speedbowl at Uniontown, Pennsylvania, on June 19, 1922, and turned a lap in 44.4 seconds—92 miles per hour.

Fronty-Fords won countless races and set innumerable track records from 1921 to 1941. Arthur and Louis Chevrolet's little company contributed more to Ford's racing successes and prestige during those years than any other—including Ford itself!

Peak Performance

For more than 80 years, climbing Colorado's Pikes Peak against the stopwatch has been one of auto racing's most

Noel Bullock power slides his homebuilt Model T special through one of the Pikes Peak hillclimb's many switchbacks on his way to a surprise 1922 win. *Artemis Images*

Bullock's fragile-looking little hillclimb champ on display in recent years. The short-wheelbase car weighed only 975 pounds. Its Model T cylinder block wore a Rajo OHV head and was set extremely low in the chassis. Bullock replaced the stock Ford planetary transmission with a Warford gearbox and floor shifter. The wire wheels are Daytons. *Artemis Images*

thrilling spectacles. Although Model T–based specials were always underdogs there, they posted two consecutive wins at the famous event.

Glenn Schultz, a Pikes Peak champion, learned to go fast on the tricky 12.4-mile dirt-and-gravel mountain road behind the wheel of a T special. In 1921 he won the Event-1 class (limited to cars with 183-ci engines), charging to the top in 21 minutes, 54 seconds. Schultz finished slightly more than 2 1/2 minutes behind King Rhiley's Hudson special, which won the Penrose Trophy, the event's premier award.

For the 1922 Pikes Peak event, Noel Bullock surprised everyone by winning the Penrose Trophy in his homebuilt Model T special with the outstanding time of 19 minutes, 51 seconds. In doing so, Bullock beat Rhiley's second-place Hudson to the 14,100-foot summit by nearly 15 seconds.

Bullock's bobtail racecar featured a shortened (83-inch) wheelbase and weighed only 975 pounds. Its standard Ford cylinder block was topped by a Rajo OHV head. The internals were mostly standard, with only a special camshaft and aluminum pistons replacing the heavy cast-iron Ford slugs. A Bosch ignition distributor replaced the flywheel magneto, along with a Willard aircraft-type storage battery and Champion spark plugs. The hillclimb powerplant was set very low in the frame, allowing only 4 inches of ground clearance. An oversize radiator required no fan or water pump.

Getting to the top of Pikes Peak requires careful gearing, so Bullock replaced the Ford two-speed planetary transmission

Lora Corum's stunning fifth-place finish in the 1923 Indy 500 inspired the Barber-Warnock Ford team to return to the Brickyard with three cars in 1924. Period cameras had difficulty capturing Bill Hunt in high-speed action in 1924. *From the collections of The Henry Ford*

with a beefy Warford six-speed, sliding-gear-type gearbox with conventional floor shifter. Special external-contracting service brakes helped slow the car on the corners, and lightweight Dayton wire wheels covered by 28x3-inch Firestone cord tires provided the grip.

Fronty-Fords Shock Indy

For a racecar owner in the 1920s, an entire season's potential winnings from dirt- and board-track events couldn't come close to a single victory at the Indianapolis 500. The famed Brickyard had become the world's most important and richest motor race, paying $20,000 to win, $10,000 for second, and $100 for every lap led. (By comparison, Babe Ruth, the highest paid professional athlete in America, earned $52,000 per

year from 1922 to 1926. The average pro baseball player at the time was paid $7,000, the average worker made $1,500, and a new Model T Roadster cost less than $300.)

Such high purses at Indy, along with the general auto-racing boom across the country, sparked the rise of specialist racecar builders. The Chevrolet brothers' Frontenac company was one, but Harry Miller and the Duesenberg brothers built the dominant machines of the era. Powered by high-revving DOHC 32-valve, straight-eight engines, the fast, feared, and exquisite Miller and Duesenberg cars were the pinnacle of 1920s auto-racing technology.

But the best came at a high price. A rear-drive Miller 91 cost $10,000, and a spare engine was $5,000. Only the wealthiest teams could afford them, prompting some Indy

GIANT KILLERS

Model T–based racers at the Indianapolis 500

Year	Finish Position	Driver	Sponsor	Engine Type/ Displacement (ci)	Chassis	Qualifying Speed (mph)	Starting Position	Laps (200 total)
1922	17	C. Glenn Howard	Frontenac-Ford/Chevrolet	Fronty-Ford I4/181	Ford T	83.9	21	165
	19	Jack Curtner	Frontenac-Ford/Jack Curtner	Fronty-Ford I4/181	Ford T	N/A*	27	160
1923	5	L.L. Corum	Barber-Warnock Ford	Fronty-Ford I4/122	Ford T	86.65	7	200
1924	14	Bill Hunt	Barber-Warnock Ford	Fronty-Ford I4/122	Ford T	85	19	191
	16	Alfred E. Moss	Barber-Warnock Ford	Fronty-Ford I4/122	Ford T	85.2	20	177
	17	Fred Harder	Barber-Warnock Ford	Fronty-Ford I4/122	Ford T	82.7	22	176
1925	21	M.C. Jones	H.J. Skelly	Fronty-Ford I4/122	Ford T	88.4	21	33
1926	25	Jack McCarver	Hamlin Front Drive/Chevrolet	Fronty-Ford I4/90**	Ford T	86.4	25	23
1930	13	Chet Miller	Frontenac/Tom Mulligan	Fronty-Ford I4/176***	Ford A	97.3	15	161

* Curtner was allowed to start in last position without qualifying because the car had been previously wrecked in practice by Tom Mulligan.

** 1926 was the first year of the 1.5-liter (91-ci) formula. Minimum car weight was 1,322 pounds.

*** In 1930 the Indy 500 formula changed to 6.0 liters (366 ci). Minimum car weight was 1,750 pounds.

Sources: Indianapolis Motor Speedway; Indy: 75 Years of the Greatest Spectacle in Racing by Rich Taylor.

racers to invest in twin-cam Fronty-Fords for less than one-fourth the cost.

The results from a six-year period at Indy (see above) show that while the Fronty Ts had little hope of winning, they could outlast the world's fastest racecars and actually beat many of them across the finish line.

In 1922, Glenn Howard qualified his Chevrolet brothers–sponsored Fronty-Ford at nearly 84 miles per hour—roughly 16 miles per hour slower than the Miller of pole-sitter (and eventual winner) Jimmy Murphy. Jack Curtner's Ford was allowed to start the race at the very back of the grid (27th) without qualifying by virtue of his car having been wrecked in practice by another driver.

Both Howard and Curtner's Indy cars were built on moderately tweaked Model T frames, with semi-elliptic front leaf springs. Remarkably, the racers used Ford planetary transmissions, and their rear axles were also standard Ford but used special high-strength forged shafts. Both cars were

still running in the end, Howard's car the first Ford home in 17th place.

For the 1923 Indy 500, new regulations reduced engine displacements from 183 ci to 122 ci. Although only one Fronty-Ford took part in this race, it scored the best finish for any T-based car ever campaigned at the Brickyard. It also was the highest placing of any Ford-engined car until 1963, when Jim Clark's Lotus-Ford placed second.

Driven by Lora L. (known as L. L.) Corum, prepared by Arthur Chevrolet, and sponsored by the local Ford dealer, this car was known as the *Barber-Warnock Special*. By virtue of qualifying at 86.65 miles per hour, Corum started in seventh position. Tommy Milton's Miller (the eventual race winner) had qualified on pole at 108 miles per hour.

Corum's Ford was superbly prepared, and when the green flag dropped he drove a perfect race. No tires were changed, Corum was the last to pit for fuel, and he was one of the few drivers in 1923 who finished the 500 miles without

The glorious Frontenac DOHC 16-valve cylinder head crowned Fred Harder's 1924 Barber-Warnock Indy entry. Note the fabricated square-tube intake manifold and the curious use of a single updraft carburetor—most race "Frontys" used twin downdraft carbs. The head conversion's high-pressure oil and water pumps, magneto, and camshafts were all chain-driven by a crankshaft extension unit. A full-race Fronty T engine could deliver well over five times the horsepower of the stock Ford. *IMS Photo*

being relieved by another team driver (a practice allowed by the rules at the time). He averaged 82.58 miles per hour.

While the four cars ahead of Corum at the finish were all Millers, those behind him were equally elite—seven Millers, three Mercedes, four Bugattis, three Packards, and a Duesenberg.

The Ford clearly was the crowd favorite. "When Corum crossed the finish line he drew the loudest and longest roar of applause ever heard at the Speedway," noted Griff Borgeson in *The Golden Age of the American Racing Car.* "After all, out of the 150,000 spectators there were more than a few passionately partisan Model T owners and boosters, and

they all roared themselves hoarse every time the steady little underdog ticked off another lap." Corum's fifth-place finish was worth $3,000 in prize money.

The giant-killing *Barber-Warnock Special* was based on a shortened (98-inch) Model T chassis riding on stock Ford transverse springs. It also used a Ford planetary transmission and rear axle, fitted with a 3.25:1 final drive. The engine wore an OHV Frontenac R cylinder head, aluminum pistons, twin Zenith carburetors, and a Vertex-Scintilla magneto. Compression ratio was a then-zoomy 8:1.

With a 3.11x4-inch bore and stroke, the 122-ci engine reportedly produced 80 horsepower at 4,000 rpm—four

The Barber-Warnock team prepares for the 1924 Indy 500. The cars were meticulously prepared and beautifully turned out. The track's wooden pagoda, destroyed years later in a fire, stands in the background. *From the collections of The Henry Ford*

times the output of a stock Model T. To boost its durability in the grueling race, the engine was fitted with gear-driven oil and water pumps.

Corum's 1923 Indy performance induced his sponsors to enter three *Barber-Warnock Specials* in the 1924 speed fest. Unfortunately, Corum's fifth-place Ford ride had also attracted the attention of Fred and Augie Duesenberg, who hired the driver for their factory team. And he didn't disappoint, qualifying on pole at 93.3 miles per hour and winning the race.

Without their star of the previous year, the 1924 Barber-Warnock team of Bill Hunt, A. E. Moss (father of the great British racer Stirling Moss), and Fred Harder came to Indy with Fronty-Fords, Harder's fitted with DOHC cylinder heads. Due to the faster competition, they were unable to finish in the money. It was definitely a let-down for the Ford fans. Plus Henry Ford was serving as the race's guest referee that day. Nonetheless, the team's 14th-16th-17th finish again proved the reliability of the modified T drivetrain.

Later Indianapolis 500 champions cut their racing teeth in Fronty-Fords. Frank Lockhart (1926 winner), Louis Schneider (1931 winner), and the great Wilbur Shaw (1937, 1939, and 1940 winner) all piloted highly tuned Ford Ts to regional glory before hitting the big time.

Because Indianapolis further reduced the displacement limit to 91.5 ci for the 1926 500-mile race, no Fronty-Fords were entered. Arthur Chevrolet instead brought the unique *Hamlin Special*, a front-wheel-drive racecar using many Model T components.

The *Hamlin Special* was designed to compete against the $15,000 front-drive Millers at much lower cost. It used a Ford block sleeved down to 2 7/8-inch bore, with a short-stroke (3 1/2-inch) crank. It inhaled through a Frontenac 16-valve cylinder head and Roots-type supercharger. A Bosch distributor provided the spark.

Its engine was reportedly capable of 6,000 rpm—sky-high revs that must have shocked the T's original

After Corum's high placing in 1923, Henry Ford agreed to serve as grand marshall of the 1924 Indy race. Standing directly behind him in this pre-race photo op is his former race driver Barney Oldfield (with cigar). To Oldfield's right is the mustachioed Louis Chevrolet, one of the founders of Frontenac. Edsel Ford stands two men to the left of Oldfield. *From the collections of The Henry Ford*

designers! A Ford planetary transmission put the power to the pavement, and the car rode on stock Ford transverse leaf springs.

Jack McCarver qualified the *Hamlin Special* at 86.4 miles per hour, earning the 25th spot on the starting grid. But a blown connecting-rod bearing on lap 22 forced him to retire the innovative car.

When the rules for the Indy 500 were revised in 1930 to encourage the use of less-expensive production engine blocks (allowing displacements up to 366 ci), Fronty-Fords reentered the scene. Chet Miller got his first taste of the bricks in a racecar consisting of a 176-ci Fronty-headed Model T block installed in a Ford Model A chassis. Miller qualified it at

97.3 miles per hour, the fastest yet for a T-based Indy car, gridding him on the outside of row five.

Miller was maintaining an average race speed of close to 100 miles per hour when he was forced to pit for 41 minutes on lap 92 to replace the car's front leaf spring. Lacking a spare, Miller's pit crew ran into the Indy infield and found a spectator's Model T sitting alone. They proceeded to unbolt the car's front spring, then installed it in the racecar! Miller completed the race and, as legend has it, the crew swapped the spring back into the donor T before its owner returned.

Miller finished 13th, ahead of six Duesenbergs and four Millers. As it turned out, the average speed of winner Billy

If ever a Model T rod was a masterpiece of subtlety, it's this beauty. Gabby Garrison built and owned a modified roadster almost exactly like this way back in 1933 and reprised it more than 60 years later. With 20-inch-diameter Buffalo wire wheels and Essex steering, the re-creation rides lower and steers more precisely. And its "souped up" engine gives it plenty of pep. *Dain Gingerelli*

Arnold's Miller-engined Summers was just a whisker over 100 miles per hour. But Arnold's car cost far more than the $3,000 Chet Miller had in his Fronty-Ford!

Birth of the Hot Rod

By the early 1930s, Ford's Model A, the six-cylinder Chevrolets, and their competitors had taken over as America's most popular cars. The Model T was obsolete and worn out. Old flivvers were filling up junkyards and being left behind barns to rust away by the tens of thousands. As the Great Depression worsened, the T became the automotive symbol of economic hardship. It was widely seen as a jalopy for people who couldn't afford anything better.

A few ingenious, speed-crazed car nuts, whose veins coursed with gasoline, thought otherwise. They saw the T's stout chassis and narrow, compact body as ideal pieces with which to build fast, inexpensive, and raucous cars. And they could draw from a deep well of Ford tuning knowledge and speed parts.

Even more than the earlier go-jobs and Speedsters, this new breed of machine reflected owner personalities, senses of style, and mechanical know-how.

"Model Ts were really the first cars modified as what we'd call hot rods today," observed automotive writer Ken Gross, a respected hot rod historian and founding director of the Petersen Automotive Museum. "That's because the Fords were cheap and universal.

COMING FULL CIRCLE
From Ts to Rods and Back

The first chapter of the Model T Ford Club of America formed in 1965 in San Fernando Valley. Some of those who joined belonged to another group that was already 30 years old: the Throttlers of Hollywood.

The Throttlers were among more than two dozen Los Angeles–area car clubs that began appearing in the mid-1930s, mainly to organize dry lakes racing events. Along with the Road Runners, Sidewinders, 90-MPH Club, Ramblers, Night Flyers, Knight Riders, Tornados, and others, the Thottlers were interested in creatively squeezing as much speed out of their cars—mostly Fords—as possible.

Bob Cressey, barely 20 when this photo of him with his early T rod was taken, was an original member of both clubs. He was comfortable in both camps, which was fairly uncommon in those days. The traditional Model T owner at the time was generally interested in keeping flivvers original, having great disdain for the sacrilegious hot rod and custom car guys who saw the T as a blank canvas.

Cressey had milled his T's cylinder head and added a Delco accessory distributor, Winfield carburetor, and a Wheeler accessory muffler cut-out after Z-ing the frame and adding an aftermarket two-speed transmission and 3:1 rear axle gears.

In 1968, the remaining Throttlers began holding a first-Sunday-in-October reunion in Burbank, California. The organizers were several of those belonging to both the Throttlers and the San Fernando Valley T chapter, so it was a natural progression for those Throttler/T club guys to ask the T club for assistance.

Ever since 1986, the Throttlers Picnic and Car Show has been sponsored by the San Fernando Valley Model T Ford Club and has taken place in its original form, with no entry fee, no pre-registration, no cost of admittance. It's a very special gathering where racers, rodders, and collectors (young and old) can bring their cars—all types are welcome—to reminisce, kick tires, and enjoy the day and one another's cars.

Hot rod pioneer Bob Cressey and his T roadster, built in the 1930s. *Bob Cressey*

Ak Miller, one of the toughest-ever American race drivers, stands next to *Cabello de Hierro*—the Horse of Iron. Miller built the T-bodied mongrel on a $1,500 budget to contest the grueling 2,000-mile Carrera Panamericana road race in 1953. The car featured an Oldsmobile Rocket V-8, Cadillac transmission, and early Ford rear end. The front grille was made of chrome-plated electrical conduit. The car was as fast as the Ferraris entered, and Miller and co-driver Doug Harrison placed eighth. The following year, with numerous mechanical upgrades, *Cabello de Hierro* placed a credible fifth. *Greg Sharp/NHRA Wally Parks Motorsports Museum*

"Before World War II there were abandoned Model T bodies all over the place," Gross explained. "You could buy a T for $5—or less."

Veteran California rodders recall finding derelict, nearly rust-free Ts while driving east from Los Angeles to the dry lakes of the Mojave Desert. It was at the flat, expansive Muroc, Rosamond, Harper, and El Mirage lakebeds in the early 1930s where kids began running hopped-up cars as fast as they could go, although the nascent hot rod phenomenon was by no means exclusive to Southern California.

Besides its availability and low cost, the T had other attributes as a hot rod platform. Its body tub, particularly the svelte turtledeck Roadster's, looked great. Unlike some cars, the T's windshield didn't require chopping; you simply removed the upper section. And perhaps best of all, the T was minimalist and light.

"You could get a really low silhouette when you built a T hot rod," said Gross. "When dry lakes racing began in the 1930s, guys running Model As and '32s realized that the best silhouette was a channeled T. So they built what came to be

Michael "Blackie" Gejeian built this 1926 T roadster in the late 1940s, and he still owned it in 2008. This was the first T built in the "lakes-modified" style to win the prestigious Oakland Roadster Show (1955). Power comes from a 59AB flathead bored and stroked to 296 ci and wearing an Edelbrock four-carb manifold. After sitting idle from 1979 to 1998, the car was disassembled by its 73-year-old owner and restored for the fiftieth anniversary of the Oakland Roadster Show in 1999, where it was a smash hit. *Dain Gingerelli*

known as 'lakes-modified' roadsters using channeled T bodies with a hand-formed 'track' nose for improved aerodynamics." (Channeling is a traditional rodding modification that lowers the car's body over the frame rails, thus lowering its overall height. The beautifully curvaceous "track" noses emulated those of dirt-track racecars and dramatically altered the look of the car.)

When standard-bodied Ford V-8s on alcohol fuel were running 125–128 miles per hour on the dry lakes, the same motors in channeled Ts with track noses were pushing 140!

The Model T's frame rails were reasonably sturdy, although some early rodders preferred rails taken from old Essex cars or Model As. The Essex rails were strong and had a kickup at the rear, which allowed the car to sit even lower. Since the spindly T was originally designed for a mere 20 horsepower, rod builders tossed much of the stock running gear before installing engines with far more muscle.

"The axles were worthless, although some guys used the stock T parallel leaf springs," noted Gross. "Nobody wanted the planetary transmission, and the stock T effectively had no brakes. So these all were replaced with stronger and more modern equipment from a variety of later-model cars."

607

Best wishes from one *Hot Rodder* to another
Ed Iskenderian

ED ISKENDERIAN'S FIRST HOT ROD
This T-body car was a real eye-stopper when Isky built it in the early days of Hot Rodding in 1938-39 . . . and he still has it to this day!

Legendary camshaft grinder and speed-industry pioneer Ed "Isky" Iskenderian paid $4 for his 1924 Model T roadster in the late 1930s. He swapped its unreliable Rajo-headed four-banger for a Ford V-8 with rare Maxi cylinder heads (with overhead exhaust valves), among other modifications. Isky drove this car to 120 miles per hour on the California dry lakes in 1942. "The Camfather" still owned this remarkable hot rod in 2008. It is in unrestored condition, looking just as it did when it appeared on the cover of *Hot Rod* in April 1948. *Ken Gross archive*

Spawning the Speed Shop

Early T rodders sought out many of the power ploys that Ford racers had used for years: OHV and OHC cylinder heads; Winfield or Zenith twin-carburetor setups; Delco or Bosch distributor-type ignitions; aluminum pistons; special connecting rods; counterbalanced crankshafts (some with five main-bearing conversions); and gear-driven oil and water pumps. Swapping the T engine for a hopped-up version of the later Model A or B four-banger was another alternative. With a bit of wrenching, most of it worked as well on the street and dry lakes as it did on the oval tracks.

Soon after its opening in 1923, an auto salvage yard in Bell, California (then a nondescript town in the shadow of south Los Angeles), became what was probably the first speed shop in America. It owed its inception to the Model T.

Bell Auto Parts was run by a scruffy mechanic named George Wight, whose cash flow was dominated by a healthy Ford used-parts business. At the time, dirt- and board-track racing was flourishing in the L.A. area, and the guys running Ford Ts soon found Wight to be a ready source of engine parts, axles, and other racing consumables.

Some swapped him hop-up equipment pulled off of wrecked or blown-up racecars for a deal on the Ford bits. He found plenty of eager buyers for the go-fast goodies, most of which ended up on hopped-up street cars.

Within a short time, Wight was making more money selling racing hardware than he made selling tired Model T stuff. Bell Auto Parts became a hub of the Southern California speed-parts scene. It added a machine shop, entered component manufacturing, acquired the Cragar brand, and later introduced Bell safety helmets.

Model T Goes Draggin'

Through the 1930s, the highly developed Ford four-cylinder hot rods frequently beat the much newer flathead V-8s in speed contests. After World War II, however, the U.S. aftermarket exploded with a mind-boggling array of V-8 performance goodies, followed by the arrival of Oldsmobile, Cadillac, and Chrysler OHV V-8s (which would, in turn, effectively kill the valve-in-block flathead, at least where dry lakes racing was concerned).

The game had changed. To keep pace in the 1950s, many T-based rods were rejuvenated with V-8 "heart transplants." One of the fastest was a semi-streamlined 1927 Roadster built by Don Waite, Bobby Meeks, and Vic Edelbrock, whose company supplied special cylinder heads and a four-carb intake manifold for the car's 304-ci flathead V-8. Running on nitromethane, the *Edelbrock Special* went 192 miles per hour on the Bonneville Salt Flats.

Besides Edelbrock, Ed Winfield, and Wally Parks, many other hot rodding heroes and founding fathers of the automotive aftermarket industry owned, built, drove, and raced Ford Ts, including Ed "Isky" Iskenderian, Dean Moon, Art Chrisman, Ermie Immerso, Andy Brizio, Ak Miller, Tony Nancy, Bill Stroppe, and Phil Weiand.

As the action began to shift from the dry lakes to the Salt Flats after the war, a new type of speed contest also

This T-based machine has been called the first true dragster, which inspired the classic "slingshot" style. Originally built by Harry Lewis in the mid-1930s with a Rajo-equipped T engine and Franklin tubular front axle for dry lakes record runs, it later received a tuned Model A engine, then a Ford V-8, and was good for 124 miles per hour. In the early 1950s, drag racing legend Art Chrisman bought it and transformed the car with a lengthened chassis, Ford disc wheels, and drag slicks. With Chrisman at the wheel, it set many track records and was the first dragster to reach 140 miles per hour in the quarter-mile. *Dain Gingerelli*

Supercharged Fuel Altereds were perhaps the squirreliest, most violently accelerating drag cars of the 1960s. Combining short wheelbase, blown big-inch V-8s (often Chrysler Hemis), and minimalist bodies—Model T roadsters, Fiat Topolinos, and English Fords or Austins were the preferred choices—the quick AA/F Altereds were great crowd-pleasers. "Wild Willie" Borsch's *Winged Express* is recognized as the first Altered to use a Cal Automotive fiberglass T body, setting a popular trend. The car was the first blown Altered to run the quarter in under eight seconds and at over 200 miles per hour. *Charles Gilchrist/Gilchrist Studios*

emerged that would quickly dominate the hot rod scene. One of the first public mentions of it actually appeared in early 1939 in the following historic blurb: "Lyle Knudsen has been challenged to a drag race with a plenty-hot T Ford owned by Monte, who holds the old T record. The race will be from 40 mph up or faster."

As published in the Southern California Timing Association's newsletter, *SCTA Racing News*, the term "drag race" was new. The act, however, of pitting two hopped-up Fords against each other for a head-to-head acceleration match was already a familiar scene on the streets and on the converted airfield runways that served as the first drag strips.

The early Fords anchored drag racing in its formative years, and as the sport boomed in the 1960s, fiberglass replicas of the Model T Roadster and Roadster Pickup body tubs helped set the style for one of the most sensational and popular classes. The AA/FA (Fuel Altered) cars were essentially Top Fuel dragsters on a wickedly short (less than 109-inch) wheelbase.

Drivers of the "Altereds," as the cars were known, were thought to be partially insane because the nitro-burning 2,000-horsepower open roadsters were a handful, to say the least. Ford's turtledeck T body was one of three popular tubs (the others were Fiat's Topolino and the English Austin) that distinguished the AA/FA competitors.

"Wild Willie" Borsch's *Winged Express* was the first Altered to use a fiberglass T-bucket body made by Cal Automotive. It featured a unique plywood-and-aluminum airfoil mounted atop the roll cage to help keep the squirrelly car under control. Borsch got his nickname from driving the car one-handed, which was one reason why the torrid T was a top crowd-pleaser for more than a decade.

The other reason was that the car was a rocket. In 1967, Borsch set his first of many quarter-mile records: 8.39 seconds at 186 miles per hour. The *Express* was the first Altered to crack the 7-second/200-mile-per-hour barrier. Its blistering 7.29-second, 207-mile-per-hour record at the 1972 NHRA Winternationals made it perhaps the world's quickest and fastest Model T drag car.

Norm Grabowski's pioneering *Kookie Car* with a young admirer at an early-1960s car show. The radically raked and customized Ford, which started life as a humble 1922 Touring, starred on the *77 Sunset Strip* TV show and ignited perhaps the most popular and imitated style of American hot rod: the "T-bucket." Both the *Kookie Car* and Grabowski's *Lightnin' Bug* which begat it were cloned years later by ace rod-builder Von Franco. *Greg Sharp/NHRA Wally Parks Motorsports Museum*

The T-Bucket Trend

If you were a television-watching kid in 1959, you knew who Kookie was. You also knew his ride: a seriously raked Model T rod with a flamed paint job, wide whitewalls, a human-skull shift knob, and a gleaming four-carb Cadillac V-8. While the fast-talking, girl-chasing character Kookie (played by actor Edd Byrnes) and his wild T were actually supporting

players in the popular ABC detective show *77 Sunset Strip* (which ran from October 1958 to September 1964), they were the show's real stars for car-loving viewers.

The *Kookie Car* is a legend in the hot rod world, being widely credited with kicking off the so-called T-bucket craze. Built on drastically shortened frames, these trend-setting machines got their nickname because their open-body

Flamboyant drag-race star and part-time actor "TV" Tommy Ivo built his own T-bucket that drew heavily on Grabowski's trendsetting machines. A Buick V-8 guy, Ivo used a seriously tuned multi-carbed 402-ci Nailhead to power his roadster. Countless Ts were constructed as "buckets" in the 1960s and the style, after going dormant for years, has returned to hot rodding once again. *Dain Gingerelli*

tubs (Roadster Pickup variants were extremely popular) resembled buckets. With tall, upright windshields, cut-down radiators set way back behind a lavishly chromed front axle, and unshrouded, full-house V-8s (typically sprouting outrageous chromed headers), T-buckets brought a radical new look to hot rods, after '32 Deuce roadsters and coupes and Model As had dominated the scene for a decade.

The *Kookie Car* actually had two lives. Before it was a TV idol, the roadster was known as the *Lightnin' Bug* and was already quite famous. Built in 1955 by 22-year-old Norm Grabowski, it started out as a 1922 Ford Touring. Having shortened a Model A chassis by 6 inches, Grabowski

modified the Touring body to fit by removing its rear-seat section and then grafted on a Model A pickup bed. Sporting glossy black paint, a nearly horizontal stance, and other differences from its second life as *Kookie Car*, the *Lightnin' Bug* won its class at the prestigious Oakland Roadster Show in 1955. It also made the cover of *Hot Rod* and was featured in *Life* magazine and *Rods Illustrated*.

Soon after Grabowski's groundbreaking T landed a spot on network television, the T-bucket fad took off. Young drag racer Tommy Ivo, himself a TV star, was one of thousands of T-bucket builders influenced by Grabowski's car. With his potent Buick-powered bucket, Ivo terrorized Southern California drag strips.

Rat Fink creator and custom car visionary Ed "Big Daddy" Roth handcrafted (usually in fiberglass) a stunning portfolio of almost futuristic T-based customs that were big hits on the show circuit and in the car magazines for many years. Plastic-model company Revell saw the potential in Roth's "far out" creations and brought many of his rods to life in 1/25 scale, including the seminal 1963 *Tweedy Pie* kit pictured here. *Photo courtesy of Revell/Ed Sexton*

Some T-buckets were built for show, not for go, however. The most famous T show cars were built by the colorful genius Ed "Big Daddy" Roth. A wild-eyed, car-crazed hipster whose fiendish Rat Fink character adorned countless T-shirts, Roth was a talented custom car and hot rod builder who truly did things his own way. In 1961 he rocked the car show scene with *Outlaw*, his almost futuristic interpretation of the T-bucket.

Outlaw's painstakingly hand-formed, slick, candy-green-over-white fiberglass body created a sensation. Many of the car's visual cues, particularly its skinny motorcycle front wheels, were new to the T-rod genre. The car was a blockbuster.

Roth and his *Outlaw* caught the attention of model-kit giant Revell. The company quickly signed Roth to a deal that transformed Big Daddy's full-sized T-buckets—*Outlaw* and *Tweedy Pie*, plus other wilder and crazier custom rods—into 1/25-scale model kits. The Revell series sold like hotcakes in the mid-1960s and did much to spread the T-bucket gospel around the world.

Within the rodding community, T-buckets can be polarizing. Critics often consider them overwrought and over-adorned. "Many of them look like glorified jukeboxes," rod-building maestro Von Franco said in a 2007 salon on his stunningly authentic *Kookie Car* and *Lightnin' Bug* clones

that appeared in *The Rodder's Journal*. But many buckets also are tastefully done, as Grabowski's and Ivo's cars, or a glance through a stack of vintage *Hot Rod* or *Rod & Custom* magazines, will show.

Love 'em or not, T-buckets are certainly ubiquitous. In the early 1960s, when original Ford Model T sheet metal and chassis parts began getting scarce, manufacturers stepped in to offer fiberglass T-bucket bodies, chassis components, and, eventually, complete rolling chassis—just add engine!

Cal Automotive, Kellison, Ford Duplicators, and other companies cranked out the fiberglass tubs both for street Ts and drag cars, such as Borsch's blown Altered. A tidal wave of "kit rods" from Dragmaster, Andy Brizio (Andy's Instant Ts), Eelco, Astra, Bird Automotive, and Speedway Motors followed on their heels.

While overall fit and finish varied significantly among kit makers, affordability was a major selling point. In 1966, Bird Automotive's T-bucket kit including interior module sold for $399.95. Speedway Motors offered a KooKie Kar T-bucket kit resembling the *77 Sunset Strip* icon for just $139.

As of 2007, Speedway Motors was still selling a variety of Model T kits, including traditional roadsters and a track roadster called the Track T. Other contemporary makers

Revell sold trainloads of its "Big Daddy" Roth T-bucket model kits in the 1960s and early '70s. The *Rodfather* kit was a reissue of *Tweedy Pie*. The *Outlaw T* (kit shown at right), which graced the January 1960 cover of *Car Craft*, perfectly captured the minimalist shape of Ford's original Model T Runabout. What would Henry think? *Photo courtesy of Revell/Ed Sexton*

include Mickey Lauria's Connecticut-based Total Performance, California Custom Roadsters, and Spirit Industries.

The T-bucket hobby has always been popular because the cars are relatively inexpensive to build and deliver loads of fun for the money. Behind this passion is the National T-Bucket Alliance (NTBA), a family-oriented club of "bucket heads." NTBA has its own website and has held a national rally since 1988.

Twenty-First-Century Speedy Ts

Even after 100 years there is no end to the Model T racing saga. New chapters are constantly being written at vintage racing events, where T-based machines with speedster bodies and booming straight exhausts regularly compete—and still show their rear ends to more modern, supposedly pedigreed racecars!

Within the antique-Ford hobby, Model T Speedsters are cultivating yet another new generation of fast-flivver lovers. Amanda Hall, Sarah Zimmer, and Mike Ritsema were all part of Model T families growing up. So it's not surprising

that Michigan high school students Hall and Zimmer and college engineering major Ritsema wanted to put together homebuilt T speedsters of their own.

In fact, the speedster contingent has become a beacon for young enthusiasts in the Model T Ford clubs. The number of speedster owners attending the clubs' national rallies has been growing in recent years, according to club officials. Just like nearly a century ago, the young adults building the cars are drawn to their sporty looks and the feeling of zippy, open-air motoring in a unique machine.

After the Model T Ford Club International's 2005 tour, Hall reflected on the numerous trophies and accolades given to her green, white, and hot-pink speedster, based on a 1921 chassis. "I was tired by the end of the week because every time we'd stop anywhere, we'd get swarmed," she recalled in a *Hemmings Classic Car* profile. The same thing happens to Zimmer and Ritsema wherever they drive their speedsters.

It's something that Ed Winfield, L. L. Corum, Wilbur Shaw, and a host of other T-racing luminaries would understand.

Hot rodders of the twenty-first century have embraced the Model T, proving that the famous flivver's style and appeal are timeless. This 2005 gathering of back-to-the-roots "retro rod" Ts during Speed Week at the Bonneville Salt Flats shows a fantastic array of vintage-Ford parts—the essence of real hot rods. Except for a few modern giveaways, the scene looks almost like the 1940s. *Dicky Hunter*

SPEAKING SPEEDSTER
The Secrets of Speed Society

In 1991, Charlie Yapp wrote an article that changed his life, an article that was published in the Model A Ford *Restorer* magazine. The piece, which focused on a Model T Speedster that Yapp had built, sparked 34 reply letters from around the world.

"Every one of the letter-writers told me they'd built a Speedster, too," Yapp recalled. "That's when I realized that we all needed a group that could share knowledge and information."

So he contacted the national Model A owners' club proposing a "funnel" organization to capture the hop-up enthusiasts who were often shunned by the originality purists in many antique vehicle clubs. Soon, the Secrets of Speed Society was up and running with Yapp at the wheel.

Named after the title of a series of 1920s articles by Model T service guru Murray Fahnestock, the SOSS launched with about 600 subscribers to its lively and informative quarterly newsletter. Yapp says the subscriber list now totals 2,600, making SOSS the world's largest group dedicated to high-performance Model Ts, as well as As and Bs.

Vintage racing, and general interest in collecting old speed parts and racecars, took off in the early 1980s. The movement helped rekindle interest in Speedsters, which had been virtually dormant for decades, explained Yapp. With rare, original Fronty DOHC cylinder heads selling for $5,000 and up (when indeed they surface on the market), Yapp decided to begin manufacturing reproduction Riley two-port cylinder heads in addition to other antique-Ford speed goodies.

As the T clubs expand their road rallies and younger people enter the hobby through Speedsters, demand for go-fast components is being revived.

"Once again it's cool to build and drive a Speedster-bodied T," Yapp observed.

"You can run the wheels off a T and not worry about it," explains Steve Rossi. To gauge his Coupe's fuel level, he's mastered the art of reading the wooden measuring stick that's standard equipment for Model Ts. Modern unleaded regular fuel works fine in the Ford's low-compression engine that's been upgraded with a Bittner electronic ignition. Rocky Mountain brakes keep those 20 wild horses in check.
Steven Rossi

Chapter 7

MODEL T'S SECOND CENTURY

Collecting, restoring, and flivver fun in the Internet age

Early Ford advertisements called the Model T the "Universal Car," certainly an accurate description of the vehicle that has faithfully handled every task given it, while always returning high value to its owners. Eight decades after the last T rolled off the Highland Park assembly line, the car's appeal remains universal and strong indeed within the antique-car hobby.

There are probably as many reasons why people continue to cherish, collect, and restore the Tin Lizzie as there were Model Ts built. Some want to own a significant piece of automotive, industrial, and American history at a reasonable price, compared with many other vintage vehicles. (Henry undoubtedly would be proud that the T remains a popular value-leader in the old-car hobby.)

Others find great pleasure in working on such a straightforward, mechanically honest machine. Many also enjoy the camaraderie of Model T clubs, parading, touring, and showing their cars and trucks with others who share their enthusiasm.

And for quite a few modern-day T owners, their vehicles represent a way to get in touch with an era when life in general was slower-paced and the only "computer" in an automobile was the one between the driver's ears.

The Midwest has always been a hotbed of Model T fanaticism, with many flivvers owned by current and former Ford employees. Richard Jeryan helped design the awesome GT, so he had to buy one for himself. The GT (in 1960s Gulf livery) provides the perfect bookend to Jeryan's award-winning 1920 Centerdoor sedan—in black, of course. *Richard Jeryan*

With their glorious hardwood bodies on display, depot hacks are crowd-pleasers at any vintage-Ford gathering. Don Smith's has been a reliable long-distance tourer for many years. He reports "this is an easy antique car to own" for anyone with basic mechanical know-how. *Author photo*

"Simplicity is the big appeal of these cars—with a screwdriver, pliers, Crescent wrench, and hammer you can take 'em apart and rebuild them," explained Felix Rotter, echoing many owners interviewed for this book.

Rotter's first car, a Model T Coupe purchased for $15, carried him to machine-shop classes at the Henry Ford Trade School in the 1930s. Over the years he never lost his love for Ts. In the mid-1980s he found a 1926 Coupe completely apart in baskets. He assembled the car to running condition and, in 2007, was preparing to revitalize the old girl yet again.

For Mark Harmon, "The Model T is a piece of history you can play with—and it's a visually appealing automobile." His handsome Brewster Green 1911 Touring, nicknamed "Loose Wheel" (a play on "Lucille"), is the young dentist's first vintage car. Harmon and his wife regularly run the car on Model T club tours, where its Rocky Mountain brakes, Ruckstell two-speed rear axle, and electric starter are much-appreciated extras.

Don Smith's 1925 Depot Hack has been a companion for 25 years, carrying Smith and his family on journeys as

THE CLUB SCENE
Fun with a Capital T

Ask just about any Model T enthusiast what makes this hobby so much fun, and the answer is likely "club activities." T owners typically recommend membership in both of the two major clubs: the Model T Ford Club International (MTFCI) and the Model T Ford Club of America (MTFCA), in addition to the many regional and local T and vintage-Ford clubs that keep members' wheels turning every weekend all over the world.

The MTFCI, founded in 1952 (and generally called "the International"), is the granddaddy of Model T clubs. The MTFCA is a relative upstart, having been launched in 1965. It is focused on the American scene, although both major clubs enjoy membership in dozens of countries. The clubs host annual meetings and tours that typically bring together hundreds of cars and trucks, plus snow crawlers, farm tractors, and any T-based oddity for days of flivver frolicking.

Besides providing a rich opportunity for socializing, concours shows, and blowing out the carbon on long

Enthusiasm runs deep in the Model T clubs, with strong attendance at the national tours and at regional and local meetings. *Artemis Images*

tours, the T clubs are vital technical and historical resources. Their award-winning magazines—the *Model T Times* (MTFCI) and *The Vintage Ford* (MTFCA)—showcase interesting cars and their owners, share regular maintenance and restoration issues, and are essential conduits for the antique-Ford parts and service network.

---

short as local Fourth of July parades and as long as vacations to Michigan's Upper Peninsula. "It's been across the Mackinac Bridge, and on one big hill near Sault Ste. Marie we had to get out and push it over the crest," Smith recalled.

What does it take to keep the hardwood-bodied hauler in fine running condition? "A sense of humor and a helluva lot of work, but that's because I'm not a mechanical person," Smith admitted. "Otherwise, with a little bit of know-how, this is an easy antique car to own."

That's also the view of Gail Petipren, who found her 1913 Runabout "sitting alongside the road" during a drive 12 years ago. She and a friend disassembled the car in one day and, after some repairs, put it back together in two days.

The spunky little roadster, now painted Midnight Blue with black fenders, has since garnered 37 trophies and ribbons at various old-car events. It even survived a broken crankshaft a few years ago; a used crank purchased for $100 spins happily inside the engine today.

Affordable Vintage-Car Fun
The Model T has been the bedrock of the vintage-car hobby ever since old-car owners started getting together. Affordability and excellent parts availability, along with the deep reservoir of shared technical knowledge, have made it accessible to tens of thousands of collectors, restorers, and others looking for an easily fixed, fun old car.

PRESERVING PIQUETTE

Two of the auto industry's most historically significant factories, both Ford Motor Company landmarks, still exist. While the remaining section of the once-sprawling Highland Park plant sits unused and forlorn along Woodward Avenue, the first factory—built in 1904 specifically for Henry Ford's fledgling enterprise—is beginning a new life on the corner of Piquette Avenue and Beaubien Street in Detroit.

The iconic Piquette plant, which sat virtually unused and unchanged from 1910 (when Ford moved Model T production to Highland Park) through 1997, is now a museum, events place, and hub of activities related to the birth of Ford's Models C, K, N, R, S, and T, as well as early automaking in Detroit.

The plant, which sits on 3.1 acres, might have suffered the same neglect as its successor, or worse, if it hadn't been for the foresight and determination of Jerald Mitchell, his wife Marilyn, and a group of devoted Ford history buffs. They recognized the factory's importance and worked tirelessly to transform it into a historical museum and education center.

"I used to drive past Piquette on my way home from work," recalled Mitchell, a retired Wayne State University Medical School professor of anatomy. "I noticed many of the windows were broken or missing—not good for keeping out the weather and animals. My wife and I had become deeply interested in Ford history [since 1985; the Mitchells have lived in the Henry and Clara Ford home in Detroit's historic Boston-Edison district] and we thought Piquette had to be preserved."

So in 1997, Mitchell approached Henry Ford Heritage Association (HFHA) president, Mike Skinner, about creating a group to save the old factory. With the help of other Ford history buffs, they formed a committee to raise funds to purchase the property. Thus the nonprofit Model T Automotive Heritage Complex, known as the T-Plex, was founded. Donations

came in from Model T aficionados, Ford history buffs, and those interested in America's industrial legacy.

In early 2000, Mitchell's dream was realized. The T-Plex group acquired Ford's first purpose-built manufacturing works. In January 2003, Ford Motor Company used the Piquette plant for media events kicking off its centennial year festivities, hosting hundreds of automotive writers visiting Detroit for the North American International Auto Show.

Jerald Mitchell (left), the visionary behind preserving the Piquette Avenue plant, and T-Plex director Dick Rubens inside the historic building. *Author photo*

Touring the three-story factory with Mitchell and T-Plex director Dick Rubens is like being in a time capsule. The interior configuration is the same as in 1909. Massive timber trusses overhead still wear their original whitewash coating. There are the huge sliding doors between interior partitions that contributed (along with one of America's first factory sprinkler systems) to the building's superior fire protection. The doors still bear their original stenciled "Positively No Smoking" warnings.

The secret room on the third floor where Henry Ford and his hand-picked team developed the first Model T is no longer there, but nail holes on the floor indicate where the room's walls existed (same with Henry Ford's own desk area on the second floor).

Rubens explained that the Piquette plant has become a center of activities related to Model T and Ford company history. T-Plex hosts conferences, workshops, and car club meetings, and regularly involves school groups in the plant's educational activities. Additionally, students and a large band of T-Plex volunteers are lovingly rehabilitating the plant's windows and overall structure as part of a multiphase revitalization plan.

Now a National Historic Landmark, the T-Plex is a destination that every Model T enthusiast, Fordophile, or anyone interested in American history should visit.

"You don't have to look for needles in haystacks with a Model T," observed Steve Rossi, board chairman of the Model T Automotive Heritage Complex (called the T-Plex) at the historic Ford Piquette Avenue plant in Detroit and owner of a 1924 Coupe.

"There is no 'secret handshake' or special code to owning and enjoying these cars," he said. "Unlike all but a few of its contemporaries, you can run the wheels off a T and not worry about it. To me, the Model T represents vintage-car fun on a regular basis."

Rossi drives his Coupe year-round, often to his corporate office during the week. On weekends he uses it for runs to get breakfast and go to the hardware store, and he carries his trash to the town dump in period luggage racks mounted on the car's running boards. He and his wife also go out to dinner in the T.

Rossi noted that around his Connecticut town, he's known as "the lunatic guy that everybody stares at in the old car." At Christmas time, he strings the Coupe with festive lights and parks it in front of his house.

In 30 years of collecting and enjoying old cars—including a number of blue-chip classics—Rossi's Model T stands out as the car he's used the most, racking up a couple thousand miles of fun per year.

In 2008, it's difficult to comprehend the Model T's ubiquity during its heyday. Half of all cars on the road *worldwide* in the 1920s were Fords, a mind-blowing statistic. So where have they all gone? And how many are still in existence today?

By the late 1930s, junkyards were increasingly filled with Model Ts, as the cars became worn out or broken beyond repair. Taking their place was a new generation of used cars of all makes, with better features. During that period, the author's father purchased his first car, a clean 1928 Model A Roadster with a rumble seat, for $25. He recalled that buying a T "would've been crazy, given everything else that was cheap and available."

The massive scrap drives of World War II severely diminished the Model T population in the United States. Within four years, cars in junkyards, rusting in fields, or laid up behind gas stations and in barns were sold for scrap and dragged away by the railcar-load to feed America's arsenal of democracy.

There have been numerous estimates of how many Ts out of the 15 million built survived the war. An extensive *Look*

To his rural Connecticut neighbors, Steve Rossi is "the lunatic guy that everybody stares at in the old car." The corporate executive and vintage-car and motorcycle enthusiast drives his 1924 Coupe year-round. He puts many more miles per year on the dark-blue flivver than he does on his other more prestigious antique cars—and says he has a lot more fun in the Ford. *Steven Rossi*

magazine feature story on the Ford Motor Company in March 1952 stated that 200,000 Model Ts were registered in the United States in 1949, "more than all the autos registered when the T was created 40 years ago," the story noted.

In 1959, an *Antique Automobile* story reported approximately 25,000 Ts were licensed in the United States, although the article did not cite a source for the estimate. The so-called first wave of Model T restorations in the 1950s and 1960s, plus the T's popularity in the postwar hot rod culture (see Chapter 6), boosted the number of cars in circulation.

Some enthusiasts today reckon that 50,000 to 60,000 roadworthy Model Ts survive worldwide. Others estimate the total, including non-runners, to be close to half a million. But it's difficult to draw an accurate bead on the real universe of cars. One reason is because many owners have multiple Ts, commonly a mix of runners, parts cars, and examples "awaiting restoration," noted Gilbert "Red" Hall, the 2007 president of the Model T Ford Club International (MTFCI).

Hall explained that many Ts that survived World War II in original condition and were restored in the next two decades have been re-restored in recent years.

A Family Affair

As the Model T enters its second century, passion for the cars has crossed generations. T ownership and restoration has become a family affair. Red Hall's daughter Amanda, a recent high school graduate, picked up her dad's T bug when she began driving the family's 1926 roadster at age 12.

Recently the father-daughter team built Amanda her own speedster, with Amanda co-designing the sports bodywork, choosing the wild pop-art paint scheme, and handling many of the restoration chores. When Amanda and her friend, Sarah Zimmer, another young speedster builder from a T-loving family, proudly charge down a country lane in their low-slung Fords, no one can miss the huge smiles on the young ladies' faces.

A speedster also came naturally to Mike Ritsema. The college freshman engineering major has the same gasoline coursing through his veins as his dad, Gerrit, and granddad, Gerhard, who is known as "Jerk." The three Ritsemas are legends of the Model T hobby in western Michigan. They collaborated on young Mike's newly built speedster based on a 1923 chassis and 1919 engine, though Mike handled much of the car's construction.

If you think the Model T hobby is only for geezerly men, you haven't met Amanda Hall (left) and Sarah Zimmer—or seen their wild pair of speedsters. The Michigan ladies come from antique-Ford-lovin' families, and both were bitten by the T bug as high school students. Each put in countless hours between studying and other school activities to craft eye-popping, sweet-running speedsters for the new century. *David LaChance/Hemmings Classic Car*

Hall and Zimmer draw crowds wherever they drive their way-cool speedsters. The cars' engines were built with help from the ladies' dads, both Model T experts. The flathead mills feature a host of hot-rod tricks, including high-lift camshafts and big-bore aluminum pistons. Wanna drag? *David LaChance/Hemmings Classic Car*

"This project was a great learning experience," said Mike, adding that his college friends think the matte-black machine is cool.

As in the 1920s, speedsters are a lightning rod for the younger generation. There were 25 speedsters among 420 Ts at the MTFCI's 2006 national tour, and at least half of them were built by enthusiasts under the age of 25.

With a workshop, barn, and adjacent yard full of Model T parts, Gerrit Ritsema believes he and his dad have enough

components to assemble three or four complete cars. Jerk's phone rings constantly with calls from T owners and restorers all over the world. His usual response is, "When do you need the parts? I'll dig 'em up and send 'em out!"

The Ritsemas acknowledge that the days of spotting a T in a farmer's barn or oxidizing underneath a tree are probably gone. With a little bit of searching, though, good-running Model Ts (or those that might need a bit of

continued on page 195

Above: Speedsters have been part of the Model T lure for nearly as long as Tin Lizzies have existed. Another young enthusiast who fell for their charm is engineering student Mike Ritsema. In early 2007 he built his primer-gray *College Boy Special* using a 1923 chassis and running gear, a handbuilt plywood body, and a 1919 engine. "I haven't pushed it yet," he says of the 1,300-pound machine, "but it's pretty quick on the back roads." *Author photo*

Left: Aside from a .060-inch overbore and meticulous preparation, the 89-year-old engine in the *College Boy Special* is mainly stock. It even eschews an aftermarket water pump for the standard Ford thermo-siphon cooling system. *Author photo*

Model T hobbyists often come in families. Such is the case with three generations of Ritsemas from Zeeland, Michigan. Family patriarch Gerhard "Jerk" Ritsema (standing behind his 1923 Touring) became a T owner in 1950. He currently owns a dozen examples. Son Gerrit (in car) is an ace mechanic and vintage-Ford historian. Grandson Mike carries the family's Ford flame with his newly built speedster. *Author photo*

"Jerk" Ritsema and his friend, Pete Elzinga, in 1955, about to begin their 28-day roundtrip journey from Michigan to San Francisco in a 1919 Touring. Ritsema, then 19 years old, packed a spare short-block for insurance, but it wasn't needed. The car suffered three flat tires along Route 66 and averaged 20–25 miles per gallon. *Author photo; original photographer unknown*

Above and left: This field full of Model T axles, frames, springs, and rolling chassis is located behind a barn packed to the rafters with virtually every other component, in various conditions. Everything is serviceable, like the flywheel magnetos on the shelves in the foreground. Treasure troves like this are rare these days, but parts availability in the T hobby is strong. *Author photos*

Each February the Model T Ford Club of America's Snowmobile Chapter meets on frozen Lake George, New York, where Bill and Betty Clough are seen exercising their Snow Flier–kitted T. Snowmobile conversions are one of the most fascinating and fun elements of the Model T hobby. In 1922, Ford dealer Virgil White began offering $250–$400 conversion kits for Fords, eventually making nearly 20,000 kits between 1924 and 1929. Other companies also made the front-ski/rear-track kits that were popular in the northern U.S. states and Canada. *Daniel Strohl/Hemmings Classic Car*

Doug Hauge's wooden utility-bodied snowmobile is based on a 1920 Touring. It was originally used by a Lake Placid lodge to transport wintertime guests and their luggage. *Daniel Strohl/Hemmings Classic Car*

Model T collecting is also popular on a "reduced scale," with a broad range of die-cast models in various sizes and Ford vehicle types available from many global vendors. *Author photo*

continued from page 190

TLC before they're roadworthy) can be found (as of 2007) for around $5,000, according to T experts and respected publications such as *Hemmings Motor News* and *Old Cars Price Guide*.

Don't expect great cosmetics at that price level, but you will have the basis for a fun machine and sound restoration project. Double that price range for decent sheet metal, paint, and interior. Experts say show-quality Ts start around $15,000—less than the price of a new minivan. "Two-pedal/two-lever" cars from the first 2,500 units built through early 1909 are the most prized of all.

For a car now entering its second century, the Model T's parts backup is outstanding. Owners can choose from used parts in rebuildable condition, reproduction parts (including a variety of tires), and even some new-old stock (NOS) Ford items offered in the T-specific catalogs from many national parts suppliers.

Flea markets such as the annual Hershey, Pennsylvania, classic and the pre–World War II parts fest in Chickasha, Oklahoma, are another good source—and part of the fun of owning a Model T. Of course, the impact of eBay on the Model T hobby has been profound, said Don Lang, a lifelong T lover who quit his job as a high school shop teacher in 1981 to launch his Massachusetts-based company specializing in antique Ford parts. "Because it reflects global supply and demand, prices on eBay typically are stronger than at your local flea market," Lang explained. "On the other hand, with eBay you don't have to spend a week searching at Hershey."

Parts for pre-1913 models are naturally the scarcest, Lang said. In recent years he has paid $2,500 for a rare one-piece engine/transmission pan for his 1911 Runabout. Open-valve-chamber cylinder blocks for the 1909–1911 cars can cost up to $5,000 in serviceable condition, and it's not uncommon for rear-axle housings for pre-1913 cars to be priced up to $2,800 per pair.

Of course, consumables are the hottest-selling items for Lang's Old Car Parts, full-line suppliers, and dozens of specialty vendors (see appendix). Transmission bands and bearings, hoses, exhaust systems, wiring harnesses, suspension and steering bushings, and tires lead the list. And the selection of modern reproduction parts is staggering—Lang deals with more than 300 vendors from all over the world.

Newly made front-end sheet metal is available for all model years, as are complete wooden body structures. The quality of reproduction parts has improved measurably in the last decade, and even impresses originality purists such as the Ritsemas.

Upgrades that are unseen on the car but vastly improve its ability to cope with modern driving conditions include: lightweight aluminum pistons to replace the heavy stock cast-iron items, Watts multi-plate clutches, oil screen filters, and sealed Timken tapered-roller bearings to replace Ford's loose-ball sets on axle spindles and driveshafts.

Today's T owners swear by the near-bulletproof Kevlar linings made for transmission brake bands and rear-brake shoes. Other popular stealth modifications include electronic ignitions that reside inside the stock timer housing and Rocky Mountain brake kits that are made again today.

The long-wearing Kevlar bands cure one of the T's original design flaws: cotton debris from the stock band-linings ends up in the sump, which is then carried into the oil line leading to the engine's number-one main bearing. A clogged oil line can cause bearing failure. Today's owners and restorers know that Ford's splash-lubrication system puts the number-one bearing at risk of oil starvation when the car is climbing long grades. Many California-bound travelers discovered this the hard way on Route 66 in the 1930s.

With more than a dozen Model T cars and trucks in its fleet, The Henry Ford's is the world's largest operator of the famous Fords. The Ts, including this 1916 Tourer, run seven days per week, when Greenfield Village is in season, hauling tourists, carrying cargo, and handling various chores around the famous Village. Keeping the flivvers flyin' is a dedicated team of experts, including full-time antique vehicle specialist Ken Kennedy (kneeling) and volunteer mechanics Bruce Phillips (standing at left) and Chuck Mitchell. *Author photo*

Because toting tourists is the primary job of the Greenfield Village Ts, most of them are five-passenger Tourers. The fleet also includes a six-passenger depot hack currently in use, plus another being restored. *Author photo*

Mechanic Bruce Phillips oils a front-axle kingpin, part of the Village's rigorous maintenance protocol that begins early every morning. Each car racks up 8,000–10,000 miles per year. "It's a real tough duty cycle," says Ken Kennedy. "Most of the driving is in low gear, and the cars are fully loaded with up to six passengers." *Author photo*

New Ts for Ford's 100th

When Ford began planning its 2003 centennial celebration, company leaders decided to pay homage to its most famous product by building a small batch of brand-new Model Ts.

And why not? Copies of the car's blueprints, including subsequent engineering changes, are archived in the fabulous Benson Ford Research Center in Dearborn, Michigan. Ford

One of the six Centennial Ts under construction in a dedicated Ford Motor Company specialty-vehicle build shop. The project was launched in 1999 and cost approximately $200,000 per car. *Ford Motor Company*

is a world leader in computer-aided vehicle development, including the rapid-prototyping tools that are key to low-volume, specialty-vehicle programs. And the automaker had no trouble finding engineers eager to resurrect the car that put the world on wheels.

The ambitious project, called T-100, was kicked off in 1999. Ford engineer Bill Leland and Guy Zaninovich, a former maintenance technician of The Henry Ford's operating fleet, were assigned project manager and technical leader, respectively. Their aim was to build six Tourers to 1914 specification, replicating as much as possible the original processes used by Henry Ford's small development team.

The 1914 model year was chosen because it was the first vehicle built on Ford's moving assembly line; the first of the "any color as long as it's black" production; and the first built by workers paid Ford's revolutionary $5 daily wage.

Leland's group decided to produce a number of major components, including new frames, cylinder blocks and heads, and various chassis bits, in Ford's prototype shop. Bodies were provided by a Model T specialist in Sweden.

continued on page 203

GOING HOME AGAIN
A special Model T's 80th birthday
By Bryan Ostergren

Author Thomas Wolfe wrote, "You can't go home again," but I suggest that you shouldn't believe everything you read. Had I believed Mr. Wolfe, I would have missed out on one of the more enjoyable experiences of my life, and "Old Charley," a "barn fresh" 1922 Touring, wouldn't have been able to spend its 80th birthday returning to the old homestead where it had spent the first 60 years of its life.

Given that Old Charley had to leave home before it could go back, it might be best to start at the car's birth. Old Charley rolled off the Highland Park assembly line late in the 1922 production run. Its engine assembly date is July 26, 1922. One week later, Old Charley arrived at the Stapp Ford agency in Newport, Kentucky, across the Ohio River from Cincinnati.

Charles Braun, a young farmer, made the 14-mile trip up Highway 8 from his farm to Stapp Ford to buy a new car. Braun opted to spend the extra $25 for demountable rims, but apparently had better things to do with $70 than spend it on an electric starter and generator.

Given Ford's pricing at the time, he likely paid around $375 for the car. But the original bill of sale lists the purchase price as "one dollar and other considerations." I've been told that was, and still is, a common practice for listing a purchase price (for tax reasons). August 2, 1922, found both Charleys heading back down Highway 8 to the Braun farm where together they would spend the next 60 years.

Old Charley emerges from his long slumber. This scene is the dream of every antique-vehicle collector. *Bryan Ostergren*

As his new Ford represented a sizeable investment, Braun took good care of Old Charley. When not in use, the car was kept under cover, parked in a large shed across from the barn. The Ford was driven to town once each week so the family could attend church services and get supplies, and occasionally to the nearby town of Alexandria. Braun claimed that he even drove the Model T to Cincinnati (about 35 miles roundtrip) twice!

Old Charley wasn't taken out in bad weather or when there was snow on the ground. That's what the horse and sleigh were for.

Probably the hardest use Old Charley saw was the drive from the shed out to Fender Road and back. The farm buildings stood about a quarter-mile off the road, down a narrow, winding dirt lane through the woods. Much of the time it would have been negotiated in low pedal with the body and frame flexing quite a bit. Over time, one of the transmission support arms broke and low gear became noticeably noisy. Even so, the old Ford was well cared for and was serviced whenever it was needed at Fender's Garage in nearby Melbourne.

At some point young Charley Braun must have grown tired of cranking Old Charley and installed a starter. Originally wired for magneto-powered headlights (as were all non-electric-start Ts), Old Charley also acquired the full wiring harness of a starter-generator car—except that none of the wires were ever connected. Today the ignition/light switch part of the loom pokes through the firewall and just lies across the steering column. Perhaps Braun started to convert the Ford but never quite got around to finishing the job.

The only other additions to Old Charley were an APCO steering column brace, an APCO fan-belt guide, and a pair of rearview mirrors.

In 16 years of service, Braun put around 8,000 miles on the Ford before retiring it to the back corner of his shed. The last year Charley was registered was 1938.

Even in retirement Old Charley was valued and looked after. A niece of Braun's remembered attending a family get-together at the farm in the fall of 1940. She recalls sitting on a farm wagon in the shed and looking at Old Charley resting in the corner while listening to a battery-powered radio broadcasting the Cincinnati Reds playing in the World Series. She was even admonished not to touch the car. And she remembers that Old Charley's paint was still shiny and black.

As the years passed, Charley remained in the corner, collecting dust. It was early in April 1982 when Bud Scudder, a Model T Ford Club of America member from California, Kentucky, heard a coworker mention that he knew of an old farmer with an old Model T parts car sitting in his barn. Of course, Bud figured it would be worth a look. Besides, it was only about 10 miles away.

Arrangements were made and Bud paid a visit to the then nearly 90-year-old Charley Braun. From that very first look at the old Ford, Bud could see that this was no parts car. Old Charley was resting on its rims; all four tires had been removed at some point. The Model T was sitting a bit twisted with its left rear wheel in a hole carved out by water flowing downhill through the shed. But a closer inspection showed there wasn't even a ding on the body.

An old burlap fertilizer sack sat across the top of the left front fender. Bud pulled it off, revealing a jagged hole that the leaking fertilizer had eaten through the metal. Other than that, all four fenders were perfectly straight. The upholstery was weathered and worn but reasonably intact, as was the top. Forty-four years of settled dust in that very humid climate had taken its toll on the paint, with only scattered patches of black mixed with surface rust. But a quick tug on the crank revealed that the engine was still free. Bud decided he wanted that old Ford.

A price was discussed. Braun had a figure in his mind. Ben commented that he thought that was a bit high. Braun pointed to his Chevy pickup replying, "I thought $6,000 was too much to pay for that truck. But that's what I had to pay." That logic left no room for negotiation, so the deal was made.

Bud returned on April 15 with a truck and trailer, his son Rick, son-in-law Mike, and friend Tom Lawton to retrieve Old Charley. Using come-alongs, Old Charley slowly emerged into the daylight for the first time in 44 years. Once the Ford was chained onto the trailer, Braun climbed up in the front seat for one last ride out to Bender Road.

The next day Bud received a phone call from a friend in Ohio. "I heard what you did!" This friend had known about the Ford and had been trying for some time to buy it. Bud would find several other locals who also had been after the car. For whatever reason, Bud had been lucky enough to come along at just the right time.

It just seemed right to Bud to name the Ford Old Charley, and once home, he wasted no time getting the scrappy T running again. He sanded the corrosion off the points, checked the coils and found three of them were still good. He pulled the cylinder head and lapped in the valves. Fresh fluids, one new coil, and Old Charley was running again.

Not willing to wait until they could be shipped to him, Bud made a quick drive to Ohio to buy a set of tires. The next day Old Charley was back on the road.

A couple of weeks later, Bud drove Old Charley back to visit Braun. The grizzled farmer took one look at his old Ford and, apparently forgetting that he'd spent decades seeing the car resting on its rims, asked, "What'd you do to it? It's bigger than it used to be!"

Bud made occasional trips back to the farm to visit with Braun. He would ask questions about the old Ford and gradually the two men developed a friendship that lasted until Braun passed away about two years later.

Bud and his family used and enjoyed Old Charley. At the first event Bud attended with the car

that spring, an old farmer in overalls eyed the T. With a tear in his eye he told Bud, "That's the way they looked when I was a kid." Bud had already thought about keeping Old Charley pretty much the way he had found it and that comment convinced him not to change a single bolt if he didn't have to.

Bud and Old Charley were on their first tour together in 1982 through the southern part of Kentucky. They were following a watermelon truck that stopped suddenly. Avoiding a collision meant Bud locked up old Charley's wheels and a nice loud "crunch" could be heard from the T's rear end as the Babbit thrust washers gave out.

Bud hooked Old Charley up behind his friend George Coon's T and they slowly towed Old Charley into a local machine shop. When the rear axle was pulled and disassembled, they found red inner tubes wrapped around both of the axle shafts. This revelation was greeted with one wag's comment that that must have been one heck of a tire blowout!

It was obvious that the rear end had previously been apart, but inserting the inner tubes had turned out to have been successful at keeping the gear oil in the differential. With new bronze thrust washers installed, Charley was once again back on the road in short order.

Over the next few years, Bud pretty much "drove the tires off" of Old Charley as they toured Kentucky, West Virginia, Ohio, and Indiana, and even driving the old Tourer to Dearborn, Michigan, and back, along with a lot of local trips. In all, Bud figures he must have put at least 25,000 miles on Old Charley. Other than the thrust washers, the only mechanical work Bud performed was swapping out the iron pistons for aluminum ones.

In the late 1980s Bud acquired several more Model Ts, including one original 1917 Touring that he discovered while on a club national tour around Pueblo, Colorado. The car was still owned by the granddaughter of the original owners. Coincidentally, that original owner was a Scudder—but that's a whole different story. As Bud's collection grew, Old Charley was on the road less and less.

I've been involved with brass cars and Model Ts since I was 12 years old (in 1968). My dad collected cars, Model Ts in particular, and the acorn didn't fall far from the tree. I purchased my first T in 1975 and then bought three more in reasonably short order. By the mid-1990s I had developed a real appreciation for "barn fresh" condition Ts. There is just something about the look and character of a truly original car that appeals to me.

Bud and I met while on the MTFCA's Great Bend, Kansas, National Tour. He was driving his original, unrestored 1917 Touring, which, by this time, was wearing a couple of feed sacks for front seat upholstery. I was driving my TT dump truck with my buddy Oluf's 1911 Excelsior motorcycle strapped down in the bed. Our vehicles attracted each others' attention and we got acquainted.

The following year Bud and I met again on the MTFCA's Post Falls, Idaho, National Tour. I must have been drooling at Bud's 1917, for he took pity on me and mentioned that he had an original '22 Touring, too. He was planning on selling that '22—Old Charley—because of a lack of space. As Bud told me about Old Charley's history, well, it was all I needed to hear. We shook hands on the deal then and there.

Since acquiring Old Charley in 1999, Charley and I have been on four national tours and one regional, and countless local trips and errands. I've tried to stick to Bud's philosophy of leaving an old car untouched. But, given that much of my driving is in Southern California traffic, a couple of concessions to safety seemed appropriate: the addition of outside brakes and safety glass. Even with some necessary mechanical work, Old Charley is pretty much the same as the day when Bud pulled him out of hibernation.

But early in 2002, it occurred to me that I ought to do something special to commemorate Old Charley's 80th birthday.

Bud knew that even though the Stapp Ford agency had long been out of business, the building was still standing. Local residents confirmed that Braun's farm was intact although abandoned since 1984. It all got me thinking how much fun it would be if, 80 years to the day from when Old Charley rolled out of Stapp and down to the farm, we could do it again.

As Bud and I had become good friends, I knew I could enlist his help. Indeed, Bud figured that if I wanted to bring Old Charley 2,000 miles in order to be able to drive him 14 miles, why not?

So Bud contacted the company now residing in the old Stapp agency. They opened the garage doors so Charley could once again drive out of the building. Then a little detective work at the county courthouse netted another exciting discovery. The current owners of the Braun farm, Dr. Judy and Ed Neff, were very interested in knowing more of the history of the place and welcomed us to visit the farm. The Neffs promised to clear some of the brush and be there to welcome Old Charley back home.

All that remained was for me to get Old Charley back to Kentucky. Driving the car from California would have been a great adventure, but realities of life and job dictated that I use a trailer. Arriving in Kentucky, Old Charley and I drove into Newport with Bud and Ginny Scudder following us in their 1917 T. We arrived at the old dealership building about 9 a.m.

We spent an hour taking photographs and visiting with various tenants of the building. Everyone seemed quite interested in what we were doing. Then we drove out through the garage doors and headed out to Highway 8. The heat and humidity were stifling, so I pushed Old Charley down the highway considerably faster than he had done it 80 years earlier.

As I drove, I wondered what the young Braun might have been thinking and feeling in his first trip in the car. We made a stop in Melbourne to take pictures in front of the former Fender's Garage where Old

Charley had been serviced so many times during his time with Braun. Then we continued on south, turning up Fender Road toward the old Braun farm.

The lane through the woods was quite bumpy. It was strictly low-pedal driving all the way. We came into a clearing and there, uphill and to the right, sat the old homestead with the barn on the left and Old Charley's shed on the right. The farmhouse was farther up the hill. As we continued up the hill, Old Charley and I drove past the shed. The drive then curved such that Old Charley was in just the correct position to back into the shed—just as it had been done hundreds of times before.

After getting acquainted with the Neffs, we spent the better part of an hour looking around and taking pictures. The hill up to the house is quite steep—so steep and rough, in fact, that I couldn't drive Old Charley up the hill—even in reverse! Bud recalled that old Mr. Braun had told him that he preferred to walk down the hill backward because facing forward his feet would hurt as his toes would jam into the front of his shoes.

While the farmhouse had deteriorated quite a bit in the 18 years since Braun died, Old Charley's shed was very much like its former occupant—weathered and showing its age, but still in sound condition. Old Charley certainly looked right at home. There really wasn't much of anything that would suggest it wasn't August 2, 1922, all over again.

On the way home to California, Old Charley got to spend a couple of days in northern Minnesota exploring dirt roads and snowmobile trails, and in Wyoming traveling out on some desolate range land. The whole trip was a wonderful experience, visiting with old friends, making new ones, and reliving a piece of the old Ford's history. I'm extremely grateful to everyone involved for their help and cooperation and for not telling me I'm nuts for doing it.

Now that I'm back in Southern California, I'm beginning to think that 2,400 miles in a T isn't all that long a distance, as long as I can get out to stretch my legs once in a while. And August 2022—Old Charley's 100th birthday—isn't all that far off.

Hmmm . . .

Talk about patina! With Old Charley's upper windshield tilted at a wind-cheating angle, new owner Bryan Ostergren prepares to leave Stapp Ford on the long journey home. *Bryan Ostergren*

A Centennial T body prepares to meet its chassis. The Touring bodies were sourced from a specialist maker in Sweden. Six were used on the cars and four were held in reserve. The project's engineers and skilled tradesmen worked off of copies of original Model T blueprints archived in the Benson Ford Research Center at the Henry Ford in Dearborn. They tried to replicate the 1914 processes used by Ford, thus keeping true to The Henry Ford historical ethic. *Ford Motor Co.*

continued from page 197

Ten were built; six were used on the T-100 cars, and four were extras.

"It was remarkable how many of the 700 items for the T-100 project were sourced through regular contacts in the Model T hobby," noted Don Lang, who was brought in by Leland to be the project's purchasing chief.

The cars cost approximately $200,000 each to build, and the results are truly impressive. The Centennial cars have proved as rugged and reliable as their forebears. Four are in daily use hauling visitors in Greenfield Village's expanding Model T fleet. (With 14 Ts, the oldest from 1914, the Village fleet currently is the world's largest group of regularly operating flivvers.) The remaining T-100s are displayed at Ford Motor Company locations.

"They're essentially hand-built one-offs and the finish inside and out is incredible," observed Malcolm Collum, a senior conservator at The Henry Ford. "As our T fleet has grown since 2002, we've certainly experienced a learning curve regarding mechanical issues and maintenance schedules. But we expected that.

"Maybe we shouldn't be surprised," Collum concluded, "that our Ts, the originals, and the Centennials, really deliver service today as Henry Ford intended 100 years ago."

One of four Centennial Ts used in the Greenfield Village fleet. The "new-old" cars have proved as capable as the originals, and most daily visitors can't tell the difference. *Ford Motor Co.*

APPENDIXES

Books

Almquist, Ed. *Hot Rod Pioneers: The Creators of the Fastest Sport on Wheels*. Troy, Mich. SAE, 2000.

Batchelor, Dean. *The American Hot Rod*. Osceola, Wis.: Motorbooks International, 1995.

Bennett, Harry. *We Never Called Him Henry*. New York: Fawcett, 1951.

Borgeson, Griffith. *The Golden Age of the American Racing Car*. New York: W. W. Norton, 1966.

Bryan, Ford R. *Henry's Attic: Some Fascinating Gifts to Henry Ford and His Museum*. Detroit, Mich.: Wayne State University Press, 2006.

—————. *Henry's Lieutenants*. Detroit, Mich.: Wayne State University Press, 1993.

Cahill, Mary. *Carpool: A Novel of Suburban Frustration*. New York: Random House, 1991.

Dominguez, Henry. *Edsel: The Story of Henry Ford's Forgotten Son*. Troy, Mich. SAE, 2002.

—————. *Edsel Ford and E. T. Gregorie*. Troy, Mich. SAE, 1999.

Dyke's Automobile and Gasoline Engine Encyclopedia, 14th Ed. Chicago: Goodheart-Willcox Co., 1925.

Fahnestock, Murray. *The Model T Ford Owner*. Lockport, N.Y.: Lincoln Publishing, 1999.

Ford, Henry, with Samuel Crowther. *My Life And Work*. London: William Heinemann, 1922.

Gross, Ken, and Genat, Robert. *Hot Rod Milestones: America's Greatest Coupes, Roadsters and Racers*. North Branch, Minn.: CarTech, 2005.

Halberstam, David. *The Reckoning*. New York: William Morrow, 1986

Henry, Leslie R. *Model T Ford Restoration Handbook*. Lockport, N.Y.: Lincoln Publishing Co., 1965.

Keller, Maryann. *Collision: GM, Toyota, Volkswagen and the Race to Own the 21st Century*. New York: Doubleday, 1993.

Kimes, Beverly Rae. *The Cars That Henry Ford Built*. New Albany, Ind.: Automobile Quarterly Library Series, 1978.

—————. *Pioneers, Engineers, and Scoundrels: The Dawn of the Automobile in America*. Troy, Mich. SAE, 2005.

Lacey, Robert. *Ford: The Men and the Machine*. New York: Little, Brown. 1986.

Levine, Leo. *Ford: The Dust and the Glory: A Racing History, Vol. 1*. New York: Macmillan, 1968.

McCalley, Bruce W. *Model T Ford: The Car That Changed the World*. Iola, Wis.: Krause Publications, 1984.

Miller, Ray and Bruce W. McCalley. *From Here to Obscurity: An Illustrated History of the Model T Ford, 1909–27*. Lockport, N.Y.: Lincoln Publishing Co., 1971.

Nevins, Allan. *Ford: The Man, The Times, The Company*. New York: Charles Scribners and Sons. 1954.

Scharchburg, Richard P. *Carriages Without Horses: J. Frank Duryea and the Birth of the American Automobile Industry*. Troy, Mich. SAE, 1993.

Smith, Phillip H. *Wheels Within Wheels: A Short History of American Motor Car Manufacturing*. New York: Funk & Wagnalls, 1968.

Sorensen, Charles. *My Forty Years With Ford*. New York: W. W. Norton, 1956.

Steinbeck, John. *The Grapes of Wrath*. New York: Viking Press, 1939.

Stern, Phillip. *Tin Lizzie*. New York: Simon & Schuster, 1955.

Taylor, Rich. *Indy: 75 Years of the Greatest Spectacle in Racing*. New York: St. Martin's Press, 1991.

Watts, Steven. *The People's Tycoon: Henry Ford and the American Century*. New York: Alfred A. Knopf, 2005.

Yanik, Anthony J. *The E-M-F Company: The Story of Automotive Pioneers Barney Everitt, William Metzger, and Walter Flanders*. Troy, Mich. SAE, 2001.

Periodicals

The Antique Automobile

The Automobile

Automotive Industries

The Bulb Horn

Cycle and Automobile Trade Journal

The Engineer

Ford Times

Hemmings Classic Car

Hemmings Motor News

The Horseless Age

The Horseless Carriage Gazette

Look

Model T Times

Motor Age

The New Yorker

Old Cars Price Guide

The Rodder's Journal

Vintage Ford

U.S. Government Papers
Recent Social Trends in the United States. The President's Research Committee on Social Trends, 1933.

Model T Clubs
Both the The Model T Ford Club of America and the The Model T Ford Club International have chapters in every U.S. state, as well as international chapters worldwide.

The Model T Ford Club of America
119 Main St.
Centerville, IN 47330
www.mtfca.com
(Publishes *The Vintage Ford*)

The Model T Ford Club International
23181 Via Stel
Boca Raton, FL 3433-3933
www.modelt.org
(Publishes *Model T Times*)

Secrets of Speed Society
3860 Cain Run Rd.
Batavia, OH 45103
513-724-0700
www.secretsofspeed.com
SOSS celebrates the people, history, technology, and equipment of high-performance Model T, Model A, and Model B four-cylinder Fords used around the world for daily driving, cross-country touring, and racing.
(Publishes *Secrets: The Vintage Ford Speed and Sport Magazine*)

The 1903–1909 Early Ford Registry
c/o Floyd Jaehnert, President
1679 Atlantic St.
St. Paul, MN 55106
651-776-9859
www.earlyfordregistry.com

Model T Snowmobile Club
c/o Dave Hiltz
200 Upper Mad River Rd.
Thorton, NH 03223
www.modeltfordsnowmobile.com
(Publishes *The Snowmobile Times*)

The Horseless Carriage Club of America
P.O. Box 62
Bakersfield, CA 93302
661-321-0539
www.hcca.org
(Publishes *The Horseless Carriage Gazette*)

The Veteran Motor Car Club of America
Norm Canfield, Membership Vice-President
P.O. Box 320
Paradise, UT 84328
Tel./Fax: 435-245-7515
www.vmcca.org
(Publishes *The Bulb Horn*)

Historical Sites and Museums
The Henry Ford and Greenfield Village
20900 Oakwood Blvd.
Dearborn, MI 48124-4088
Call Center: 313-982-6001
www.hfmgv.org

Model T Automotive Heritage Complex, Inc.
(the Piquette Avenue "T-Plex")
411 Piquette Avenue
Detroit, MI 48202
313-872-8759
www.tplex.org

The Benson Ford Research Center
The Henry Ford
P.O. Box 1970
Dearborn, MI 48121-1970
313-982-6020
Fax: 313-982-6244
www.thehenryford.org/research

Museum of American Speed
340 Victory Lane
Lincoln, NE 68528
402-323-3166
www.museumofamericanspeed.com
(Displays the world's largest collection of cylinder-head
conversions and period speed equipment for Model T and
other vintage American racing engines.)

Model T Parts Sources
The following short list is aimed at giving the reader a
starting point for Model T maintenance and restoration
resources. Many, many more resources for virtually every
part and service can be found in advertisements in the two
major Model T club magazines, as well as by using Internet
search engines.

Lang's Old Car Parts
202 School St.
Winchendon, MA 01475
1-800-T-PARTS-1
www.modeltford.com

Gaslight Auto Parts
1445 South U.S. Hwy. 68
P.O. Box 291
Urbana, OH 43078
800-242-6491
Questions: 937-652-2145
Fax: 937-652-2147
www.gaslightauto.com

Mac's Antique Auto Parts
1051 Lincoln Ave.
Lockport, NY 14094
877-579-7946
www.macsautoparts.com

ACKNOWLEDGMENTS

Henry Ford couldn't have produced the Model T without his dedicated team of draftsmen, practical engineers, skilled technicians, and financial experts—and the unwavering support of his wife, Clara. Likewise, this book is the product of many who helped and supported me over the course of nearly two years, primarily my wife, Suzie.

Zack Miller and Dennis Pernu at Motorbooks should be knighted for their patience, particularly after my laptop computer was stolen during the writing phase of this project. With it went much of my work in progress, all of which had to be resurrected. Zack and Dennis, here's to you.

At the Benson Ford Research Center, my thanks go to Director Judith Endelman; Kathy Steiner, head of access services; archivists Rebecca Bizonet, Pete Kalinski, and Carol Whittaker; stack assistants Kira Macyda and Jonathan McGlone; reference librarian Linda Skolarus; and Jim Orr, the digital-imaging specialist who scanned more than 150 of the historical photos you see on these pages.

Access to The Henry Ford's mother lode of Ford history and Model Ts came through public-relations expert Kate Storey and senior conservator Malcolm Collum, as well as Model T technicians Ken Kennedy, Chuck Mitchell, and Bruce Phillips. Ford Motor Company archivist John Bowen provided background on the Centennial T project.

Research at the Detroit Public Library's National Automotive Historical Collection was assisted by director Mark Patrick and librarian Barbara Thompson. At the Wally Parks NHRA Motorsports Museum, curator Greg Sharp provided superb images of T rods and racers.

At the Piquette Avenue Model T Automotive Heritage Complex in Detroit, CEO Jerald Mitchell and director Dick Rubens guided me through one of America's greatest industrial treasures.

Special thanks to Steve Rossi and Ken Gross, as well as to Helen V. Hutchings for her enthusiasm, suggestions, and the sidebars on Robert Panish and the Throttlers car club. Helen also introduced me to Bryan Ostergren, author of the "Old Charley" sidebar.

Photographic contributions were provided by Chris Nazarenus and Michelle TerBest at Artemis Images; Jim Frenak at FPI; Charles and Shawn Gilchrist at Gilchrist Image Works; Dain Gingerelli; Kathleen Adelson at the GM Photo Archives; Richard Lentinello, David LaChance, and Daniel Strohl at *Hemmings Classic Car*; Dicky Hunter; Mary Ellen Loscar at the Indianpolis Motor Speedway Archives; Paul McLeod; John MacKichan and Bill Smith at the Smith Collection/Museum of American Speed; Walter Pietrowicz; Ron Rae; Ed Sexton at Revell-Monogram; Charlie Yapp at the Secrets of Speed Society; and William Zempel.

Others who provided invaluable resources, contacts, and time included Don Sherman, Jeff Sabatini, Skip Nydam, Don Lang of Lang's Old Car Parts, and Gilbert "Red" Hall.

Finally, the best part of writing this book was meeting and speaking with Model T owners—Ron Flockstra, John Forster, Bill Hall, Red Hall, Mark Harmon, Richard Jeryan, David P. Jones, Don "Dr. Flywheel" Mates, Gail Petipren, Gerhard "Jerk" Ritsema, Gerrit Ritsema, Mike Ritsema, Felix Rotter, and Don Smith. A loud "AaahOOOgah!" to you all.

—Lindsay Brooke
Plymouth, Michigan
November 2007

INDEX